FLAGS
of the
CIVIL WAR

FLAGS
of the
CIVIL WAR

TEXT BY
PHILIP KATCHER

ILLUSTRATED BY
RICK SCOLLINS & GERRY EMBLETON

CHARTWELL
BOOKS

First published in Great Britain in 2000 by Osprey Publishing,
PO Box 883, Oxford, OX1 9PL, UK
PO Box 3985, New York, NY 10185-3985, USA
Email: info@ospreypublishing.com

Osprey Publishing, part of Bloomsbury Publishing Plc

Previously published as Men-At-Arms 252 *Flags of the American Civil War 1: Confederate*
Men-at-Arms 258 *Flags of the American Civil War 2: Union* and
Men-at-Arms 265 *Flags of the American Civil War 3: State & Volunteer*

© 2000 Osprey Publishing Limited

This edition published in 2016 by
CHARTWELL BOOKS
an imprint of Book Sales
a division of Quarto Publishing Group USA Inc.
142 West 36th Street, 4th Floor
New York, New York 10018
USA

ISBN-13: 978-0-7858-3384-0

Editor: Chris Wheatley
Filmset in Singapore by Pica Ltd
Printed in China through World Print Ltd.

PAGE 2 The colors of the 15th New York Engineers

CONTENTS

CONFEDERATE FLAGS

INTRODUCTION

The very heart of the Confederate fighting unit was its flag, which came in a variety of designs and colours. The flag was the rallying point on the field of battle; it marked the unit headquarters in camp. In the South in 1861, at the outbreak of the Civil War, Private Sam Watkins of the 1st Tennessee Infantry Regiment recalled: 'Flags made by the ladies were presented to companies, and to hear the young orators tell of how they would protect the flag, and that they would come back with the flag or come not at all, and if they fell they would fall with their backs to the field and their feet to the foe, would fairly make our hair stand on end with intense patriotism, and we wanted to march right off and whip twenty Yankees.'

And in 1865, at the war's end, it was the furling of the defeated Confederate banners that marked the final closing of that episode in history. 'For want of strength,' sang Confederate veterans in their song *Wearing of the Grey*, 'we yield them up the day, and lower the flag so proudly borne, while wearing of the grey.'

The generally accepted jargon for the elements of flags and their components is used throughout this book. The *canton* is the square or rectangle placed on the top of the flag next to the pole or staff. A *border* is

The regulation First National Flag flies over fortifications in Charleston, South Carolina, harbour in this

1861 Harper's Weekly illustration. Note that the seven stars are arranged in the proper circle.

the flag's edging when rendered in a different colour than the *field*, the main part of the flag. *Fimbration* is the narrow edging used to separate different colours on a flag; it is often white. The *hoist* is the side of the flag next to the staff, while the *fly* is the opposite side. When, as is normal, the flag is shown with the hoist on the left and the fly on the right, this is the *obverse* or front of the flag; the side seen when the hoist is on the right and the fly on the left is the *reverse*, or rear. The staff itself is the *stave*; the metal top of the stave, usually a spearhead, an axehead or an eagle, is the *finial*; the metal cap at the bottom of the stave is the *ferrule*. Many flags have cords and tassels hanging from the finial, although this was rare among Confederate flags; collectively, these are simply referred to as *cords*. Finally, *ensigns* are national flags used on a ship, as well as the rank of a Confederate commissioned colour bearer after 17 February 1864; *jacks* are small flags flown at the bow of a ship in port; a *colour* is carried by an infantry or foot artillery regiment; a *standard* is carried by a mounted unit; a *camp colour* was a small flag used to indicate the location in camp of the unit (these seen to have seen little use among Confederates); and a *flag* is, strictly, that flown from a building or over a post and is not actually carried—although 'flag' is a generally accepted generic term for all flown cloth insignia that represent some nation or organization.

THE FIRST NATIONAL FLAG

When Jefferson Davis was sworn into office as the President of the provisional government of the new Confederate States of America on 18 February 1861 in Montgomery, Alabama, the flag that floated over the scene was that of the state of Alabama. The states which had so recently left the almost hundred-year-old United States to form their own government had no flag to represent their new nation.

The first flag used to represent the seceding southern states as a whole had a blue field with a single white five-pointed star in its centre. This flag was first displayed during the Convention of the People in Mississippi, 9 January 1861, as the flag of the Republic of Mississippi, which had been in existence for only one month. The flag was described in a widely popular song, *The Bonnie Blue Flag*, which was written by Harry Macarthy and first sung in New Orleans a short time later. Texans en route to join the Army of Northern Virginia sang the song in that city in September 1861. Although this design was used by several southern states and became a southern symbol, it was never officially adopted by the Confederacy as a whole.

Some military units also carried this flag; one was

This regulation First National Flag, one star hidden by a written description of how it was captured, was taken from an unknown Confederate unit on the Peninsula in 1862. Made entirely of cotton, it measures 31 inches by 57 inches. (Courtesy Mike Miner)

The First National Flag carried by the 2nd Regiment, North Carolina State Troops. The regimental designation has been stencilled on the hoist border, which also has three eyelet holes for attachment to the staff. The entire flag is hand-sewn. (North Carolina Museum of History)

carried by the 8th Texas Cavalry with its unit designation 'Terry's Texas Rangers' in yellow above the star.

On 9 February the new country's Provisional Congress appointed six of their members to a committee to select a new flag from among the dozens of proposals which had been submitted to the Congress. In less than a month, in early March, the committee had four proposed sample flags hung on the walls of Congress.

According to the final report of the committee to Congress, the search was a difficult one. The committee, they wrote, had 'given this subject due consideration, and carefully inspected all the designs and models submitted to them. The number of these has been immense, but they all may be divided into two great classes.

'First. Those which copy and preserve the principal features of the United States flag, with slight and unimportant modifications.

'Second. Those which are very elaborate, complicated, or fantastical. The objection to the first class is, that none of them at any considerable distance could readily be distinguished from the one which they imitate. Whatever attachment may be felt, from association for the "Stars and Stripes" (an attachment which your committee may be permitted to say

they do not all share), it is manifest that in inaugurating a new government we can not with any propriety, or without encountering very obvious practical difficulties, retain the flag of the Government from which we have withdrawn. There is no propriety in retaining the ensign of a government which, in the opinion of the States comprising this Confederacy, had become so oppressive and injurious to their interests as to require their separation from it. It is idle to talk of "keeping" the flag of the United States when we have voluntarily seceded from them. It is superfluous to dwell upon the practical difficulties which would flow from the fact of two distinct and probably hostile governments, both employing the same or very similar flags. It would be a political and military solecism. It would lead to perpetual disputes. As to "the glories of the old flag," we must bear in mind that the battles of the Revolution, about which our fondest and proudest memories cluster, were not fought beneath its folds. And although in more recent times—in the war of 1812 and in the war with Mexico—the South did win her fair share of glory, and shed her full measure of blood under its guidance and in its defense, we think the impartial page of history will preserve and commemorate the fact more imperishably than a mere piece of striped bunting....

'The committee, in examining the representa-

tions of the flags of all countries, found that Liberia and the Sandwich Islands had flags so similar to that of the United States that it seemed to them an additional, if not itself a conclusive, reason why we should not "keep," copy, or imitate it. . . . It must be admitted, however, that something was conceded by the committee to what seemed so strong and earnest a desire to retain at least a suggestion of the old "Stars and Stripes." So much for the mass of models and designs more or less copied from, or assimilated to, the United States flag.

'With reference to the second class of designs— those of an elaborate and complicated character (but many of them showing considerable artistic skill and taste)—the committee will merely remark, that however pretty they may be, when made by the cunning skill of a fair lady's fingers in silk, satin, and embroidery, they are not appropriate as flags. A flag should be simple, readily made, and above all, capable of being made of bunting. It should be different from the flag of any other country, place or people. It should be significant. It should be readily distinguishable at a distance. The colors should be well contrasted and durable, and, lastly and not the least important point, it should be effective and handsome.

'The committee humbly think that the flag which they submit combines these requisites. It is very easy

to make. It is entirely different from any national flag. The three colors of which it is composed – red, white, and blue—are the true republican colors. In heraldry they are emblematic of the three great virtues—of valor, purity, and truth. Naval men assure us that it can be recognized and distinguished at a great distance. The colors contrast admirably and are lasting. In effect and appearance it must speak for itself.'

The first hung on the chamber's walls, although not the committee's final choice, eventually became the symbol of the Confederacy as the battle flag of the Army of Northern Virginia as well as other Confederate military organizations. It featured a blue St. Andrew's Cross, or 'saltire' (or 'saltive' – the former is the older spelling), edged or 'fimbrated' in white, on a red field, with a white star representing each state on the saltire. It had been designed by Congressman W. Porcher Miles of South Carolina, the committee chairman.

The second flag was a close copy of the US 'stars and stripes' national flag, save that the stripes were made of red and blue, whilst the canton or 'union' remained blue with a white star for each state.

The third rectangular flag was described as 'a red field with a blue ring or circle in the centre'.

The fourth flag was that which was finally chosen and is now known as the 'First National Flag' of the

Confederacy. On 4 March, after giving members a chance to examine the four leading candidates, the committee recommended in its final report 'that the flag of the Confederate States of America shall consist of a red field with a white space extending horizontally through the center and equal in width to one-third of the width of the flag, and red spaces above and below to the same width as the white, the union blue extending down through the white space and stopping at the lower red space, in the center of the union a circle of white stars corresponding in number with the States of the Confederacy'.

Two men claimed to have designed this flag. The first was Nicola Marschall, a Prussian artist living in Montgomery, Alabama, who also claimed credit for the Confederate Army uniform design. He said that he took the basic form from the Austrian flag which had three horizontal stripes, the top and bottom one of red and the middle one of white. The letter suggesting this design was dated 2 March 1861 and would seem to back his claim. Marschall offered several variations of the canton placement, having it in the centre of the white stripe or against the hoist on the white stripe as well as in the traditional union location.

The other person who claimed to have designed the flag was Orren R. Smith, a North Carolinian. His design, he said, came from the Trinity, with the three bars standing for the state with its judiciary, legislative, and executive branches; the church; and the press. They were bound by the blue canton, with the stars in a circle signifying mutual defence.

In 1915 the United Confederate Veterans accepted Smith's claim, although in 1931 the Alabama Department of Archives and History produced a study done by the state legislature which accepted Marschall's claim. In fact, both men probably offered similar designs virtually simultaneously, since the fairly plain design was quite similar to that of the United States. Indeed, as seen, the committee noted in its final report that 'the mass of models and designs' for flags it received were 'more or less copied from or assimilated to, the United States flag'.

At any rate, in a hurry to get a flag approved in time for a scheduled flag raising on 4 March, the date United States President Abraham Lincoln was to be sworn into office, Congress approved the committee's findings, taking its report into the Con-

This First National Flag shows an arrangement of stars in the canton for the final, maximum number of stars used in

Confederate flags, 13. The stars are actually embroidered on the canton. (North Carolina Museum of History)

gressional journal with language unchanged. The result was that the so-called First National Flag was never officially adopted as the flag of the Confederacy by a full Congressional vote in a formal 'flag act' or bill. Nevertheless, for fully two years this flag was the one flown over official buildings and by many military units in the field. Indeed, since generally each Confederate regiment or independent battalion or squadron carried only one colour, although it was usually referred to as 'colors', the First National Flag was the only colour carried by such organizations as e.g. Georgia's Cobb's Legion.

In one respect the committee's language was rather vague: it included no proportions of the height on the hoist, or staff, to the length of the fly. Each maker was free to produce a flag of this design that best matched his or her aesthetic tastes. A study of

Confederate flags produced by H. Michael Madaus and Robert D. Needham shows that almost a third (30 per cent) of surviving First National Flags are proportioned 2:3 (hoist:fly). However, 21 per cent of these flags have proportions of 3:5, 13 per cent have proportions of 5:9, and some ten per cent each have proportions of 1:2 and 3:4. First National Flags produced west of the Mississippi River appear slightly more than the average proportioned 1:2, a proportion not at all common in English flags.

Equally, although officially the blue canton was to bear a circle of equally sized stars, in fact First National Flags came with a variety of designs, especially as additional states joined the Confederacy. By the third week of May Virginia and Arkansas added two more stars to the original seven. As of 2 July the canton had 11 stars, following the admission of North Carolina and Tennessee to the Confederacy. Missouri's addition on 28 November gave the flag 12 stars, while the final number of 13 was reached on 10 December with Kentucky's joining the Southern states.

The style of star, i.e. the number of rays, was not spelled out by Congress; however, the five-pointed star as used in the United States flag was the most common style used.

In many cases a single star, often larger than the others, was placed in the centre of the circle to represent the local state. This violated the original concept of having each star the same size to indicate the equality of the states in the Confederacy.

Many flags, especially those used by Texas units from the 'Lone Star State', had but one star in the

The Naval Battery near Manassas, Virginia, after the battle of First Manassas flew this First National Flag with the stars in the canton arranged in a St. George's Cross.

Company C. 20th Virginia Infantry, carried this variation of the First National Flag with its militia designation, 'Flat Rock Riflemen' and motto 'OUR RIGHTS' within the circle of badly faded stars. (Museum of the Confederacy)

canton. Flags with one star in the canton were carried by e.g. the 25th Virginia Infantry (which also had the state name painted in gold Roman letters around the white star); and Co. E, 6th North Carolina Infantry Regiment State Troops, which had its gold star within a gold laurel wreath and the gold Roman words 'IN GOD WE TRUST/VICTORY OR DEATH' above and below the star and wreath.

Some stars were placed in an apparently random design; some in rows as in the United States flag; some stars were formed into either a Greek or a St. Andrew's Cross; and some stars were placed in an arch, the 'Arch of the Covenant' which was symbolic of the Bread of Life, the symbol of spiritual nourishment. The latter design was used on Robert E. Lee's personal headquarters flag.

State seals were often painted onto the canton instead of sewn stars. Co. E, 1st Georgia Infantry

Regiment, for example, carried a First National Flag measuring 42 inches on the hoist and 66 inches on the fly with the Georgia state seal painted on the blue canton on the obverse side, and on the reverse seven white stars in a circle with a red scroll above and another below with the gold block words 'WE YIELD NOT TO/OUR COUNTRY'S FOES' on the scrolls. Co. E, 1st Maryland Cavalry Regiment had the Maryland state seal painted on the canton of their First National Flag, which is 27½ inches on the hoist and 46½ inches on the fly.

Materials also varied according to maker. Silk was the preferred material, and many First National Flags made by hometown ladies were of this fabric. The standard carried by Co. K, 3rd Texas Cavalry at Oak Hills, Missouri, and Pea Ridge, Arkansas, was made entirely of silk by the ladies of the company's home town. However, when the women of Tyler, Texas, made a First National Flag for Co. D, 15th Texas Infantry, they used cotton on the white bar and

stars as well as the canton, but a wool/cotton mixture for the red bars. A First National Flag captured at Pea Ridge from an Arkansas brigade was entirely made of wool flannel, with the words 'JEFF. DAVIS' worked in black velvet Roman uncial letters on its obverse.

One of the strangest First National Flags still in existence is that used from time to time by the 43rd Battalion of Virginia Cavalry, Mosby's Rangers. The unit carried out guerrilla warfare behind Union lines in Northern Virginia, and therefore rarely carried its standard into action. However, the flag, which measures 51 inches on the hoist by 114 inches on the fly, was used at Mosby's headquarters. According to a veteran some years after the war: 'Bunting was a scarcity in those days, and the blue field of this flag had been cut from the blouse [fatigue coat] of a Union soldier; the red stripes are of a fair quality bunting, while the white stripe is of unbleached cotton.'

There was also no regulation finial, cords, or stave size or colour. In practice, most units used brass or gilt spear point or halberd finials; eagles left over from before the war and captured with US Army colours were also used. Staves were left their natural wood colour. Cords rarely appeared with Confederate colours.

Military versions of the First National Flag also often had the unit designation painted or sewn on the white middle stripe.

THE SECOND NATIONAL FLAG

Hardly had the seamstresses turned out their first set of First National Flags when complaints about the emblems' appearance began to be voiced.

From the military viewpoint, the similarity between the two sides' flags led to confusion, especially at the first big battle of the war, First Manassas. 'The mistake of supposing Kirby Smith's and Elzy's approaching troops to be Union reinforcements for McDowell's right was caused by the resemblance, at a distance, of the original Confederate flag to the colors of Federal regiments,' recalled Confederate Lt. Gen. James Longstreet. 'This mishap caused the Confederates to cast about for a new ensign, brought out our battle-flag, led to its adoption by General Beauregard, and afterwards by higher authority as the union shield of the Confederate national flag.'

Civilians were also generally unhappy with the similarity between the northern and southern flags. 'There is little room for doubt that the resemblance of the Confederate flag to that of the United States renders it displeasing in the eyes of more than three-fourths of our population,' editorialized the *Daily Richmond Examiner* on 13 December 1861. 'The desire for a change in the present banner has been so generally manifested that is nearly certain that it will be made.' The newspaper's editor further suggested that the new flag should not have stars or the colours of red, white, and blue, preferring instead a gold or scarlet national emblem in the canton or centre of the field.

A Joint Committee on Flag and Seal was appointed by both houses of the first Confederate congress, and on 19 April 1862 it submitted its recommendation as a joint resolution: '*Resolved by the Congress of the Confederate States of America*, That the flag of the Confederate States shall be as follows: A red field, charged with a white saltier, having in the centre the device of a sun, in its glory, on an azure ground, the rays of the sun corresponding with the number of States composing the Confederacy.' After a great deal of debate the House of Representatives voted 39 to 21 to postpone further consideration of the resolution, which the Senate never formally discussed. Therefore, it died in Congress; and apparently few if any of these flags were made, as no physical examples exist today.

Nevertheless, unhappiness with the First National Flag continued. In the Confederate field armies the problem of a flag that looked like that of the enemy—an important objection when the colours regiments carried on the field were a major means of identification—was solved by local commanders (see

The painted letters spelling out 'ROANOKE MINUTE MEN' and the wreath have rotted away from this First National Flag carried by Co. A, 4th North Carolina Volunteers' when they were first mustered in. Note that the gold stars are painted only over the top of the gold-painted circle within the canton. This silk flag is all hand-sewn. (North Carolina Museum of History)

This small First National
Flag measures 13 inches by
20 inches. It was captured
near Nashville, Tennessee,
on 11 December 1864 from
an unknown Confederate
artillery battery.
(Smithsonian Institution)

the section on battle flags, below). Indeed, the battle flags of the Army of Northern Virginia were those most seen in the capital city of Richmond, and most influenced Confederate legislators.

Consequently, on 22 April 1863 Senate Bill No. 132 was introduced, which read: '*The Congress of the Confederate States of America do enact*, That the flag of the Confederate States shall be as follows: a white field with the [Army of Northern Virginia] battle flag for a union, which shall be square and occupy two thirds of the width of the flag, and a blue bar, one third of the flag, in its width, dividing the field otherwise.'

Passed by the Senate, the bill was introduced on the floor of the House on 1 May to a great deal of debate. One proposed motion removed the blue bar from the field and instead edged the field with red. Another suggested simply adopting the Army of

Northern Virginia battle flag, in a rectangular shape, as the national flag. In the end, however, the bill that passed the House and was agreed to by the senate described the flag as follows: 'The field to be white, the length double the width of the flag, with the union (now used as the battle flag) to be a square of two-thirds the width of the flag, having the ground red; thereon a broad saltier of blue, bordered with white, and emblazoned with white mullets or five-pointed stars, corresponding in number to that of the Confederate States.'

The Second National Flag was approved by both houses and became official on 1 May 1863. It was first used to cover the coffin of the beloved Lt. Gen. Thomas Jonathan ('Stonewall') Jackson, who had been badly wounded at the Battle of Chancellorsville on 2 May and died of pneumonia on 10 May. His coffin, draped with the new Second National Colour, lay in state in the chamber of the House of Representatives on 12 May. As a result of this connection, as well as due to the fact that both this flag and Jackson's picture appeared on the 100 dollar bill of the 2

February 1864 issue, the Second National Colour was often called the 'Jackson flag'. The pure white field also led to the Second National Flag being nicknamed the 'stainless banner'.

On 26 May 1863 the Second National Flag was designated by the Secretary of the Navy as the official naval jack, or ensign. The orders establishing the jack also spelled out the specific proportions of 2:3. A flag 54 inches in the fly would be 108 inches long with a square canton 36 inches on each side. The arms of the saltier were to be 1/4.8 the width of the canton, so on a flag 54 inches in fly they would be 7.5 inches wide. The white border on the saltier was to be $\frac{1}{22}$ the width of the canton, or in this case $1\frac{3}{5}$ inches wide. Each star was to have a diameter of 1/6.4 the canton width; they would be 5.5 inches in diameter in this example.

As it turned out, surviving examples differ widely from both the regulation flag and each other. The Second National Flag used as the standard of the 8th Virginia Cavalry measures 53 inches by 98 inches; that used by Lt. Gen. Jubal Early in his headquarters flag was 47 inches by $72\frac{1}{2}$ inches; and the headquarters flag of Maj. Gen. J. E. B. (Jeb) Stuart was 46 inches by 74 inches.

Moreover, Second National Flags were used mostly by the government on its buildings and forts and the navy on its ships; army units in the field did not as a whole take to the new flag. Indeed, First National Flags were still being used as late as the Battle of Gettysburg by some units in the Army of Northern Virginia, despite the new flag's introduction.

Some Second National Flags were apparently issued by the Richmond Clothing Depot, which made unit colours and standards as well as clothing, to units in the Virginia and North Carolina theatres, although plain First National Flags continued to be carried—e.g., by the 44th and 60th Georgia Infantry Regiments—in that theatre even after the new flag's introduction. The Second National Flags from the Richmond Depot were made of cotton and bunting in the correct 2:3 proportion. The dark blue St. Andrew's cross bore 13 white five-pointed stars. The white fimbration overlapped the ends of the cross.

In large part, however, Army of Northern Virginia units that received the new flags cut off the white field and flew only the small battle flag when on active service. As mentioned above, a number of Second National Flags were used as headquarters colours by various Army of Northern Virginia general officers, among them Stuart and Early.

Soldiers in the Western theatre, however, apparently took to the new flag more than those in the East. There a small number of infantry regiments received these flags and carried them as their regimental colours. These flags generally lacked the white overlap at the ends of the cross. The 11th

This Second National Flag bears the US War Department capture number '234' stamped in the canton. (Museum of the Confederacy)

Table A: First National Flags

First National Flags came in a variety of different sizes according to the type of unit which carried them: below are some representative sizes, in inches.

Unit	Unit type	Flag size
Border's Texas Cavalry	Cavalry battalion	$35 \times 65\frac{1}{2}$
Bully Rocks	Cavalry company	$36 \times 81\frac{1}{2}$
Co. C, 2nd Kentucky	Infantry company	57×64
Co. F, 17th Texas	Infantry company	46×67
Corinth Rifles	Infantry company	42×66
11th Texas	Cavalry regiment	$23\frac{1}{4} \times 24\frac{1}{2}$
18th Virgina	Infantry regiment	42×55
Floyd Guards	Infantry company	$47\frac{1}{2} \times 76$
Jefferson Davis Guards	Infantry company	49×76
Rutherford Volunteers	Infantry company	39×81
St. Mary's Cannoniers	Artillery battery	48×65
6th Texas	Infantry regiment	34×69
10th Texas	Cavalry regiment	$36\frac{3}{4} \times 77\frac{1}{2}$
20th Texas	Infantry regiment	53×92
21st Tennessee	Infantry company	$17\frac{1}{2} \times 36$
22nd/35th Arkansas	Infantry regiment	$19\frac{3}{4} \times 32\frac{1}{2}$
25th Virginia	Infantry regiment	49×103
Washington Rifles	Infantry company	42×66
Winder Cavalry	Cavalry company	$27\frac{1}{2} \times 46\frac{1}{2}$

Tennessee Infantry Regiment even painted its unit designation in dark blue on the field over battle honours for Rockcastle, Cumberland Gap, Tazewell, Murfreesboro, Chickamauga, and Missionary Ridge. Its colour measured $33\frac{1}{2}$ inches by 67 inches, and did have overlaps on the ends of the St. Andrew's cross. The 8th Virginia Cavalry Regiment embroidered its unit designation in white on the field, along with a battle honour for White Sulphur Springs in the same material.

THE THIRD NATIONAL FLAG

From the first day the Second National Flag was run up the flag pole, complaints were made about its appearance. The most serious one was that when limp, in a windless day, it looked like an all-white flag of truce. Many flag makers attempted to resolve this problem by making the canton disproportionately large (see Plate B1).

This did not solve the problem, however. The *Daily Richmond Examiner* suggested that since the horse symbolized the 'equestrian South', it should be used in black on a white flag as a new national flag. Indeed, the Confederacy's 'Great Seal' featured Virginian George Washington mounted on his war-horse. Although this suggested flag met some acceptance, there was also opposition, especially to giving up the battle flag, which had flown over so many hard-fought fields, as an element of the new flag.

Therefore, on 13 December 1864 Senate Bill No. 137 was introduced, specifying a new flag designed by an artilleryman, Major Arthur L. Rogers. It legislated 'That the flag of the Confederate States of America shall be as follows: The width two-thirds of its length, with the union (now used as the battle flag) to be in width three-fifths of the width of the flag, and so proportioned as to leave the length of the field on the side of the union twice the width of the field below it; to have the ground red and a broad blue saltier thereon, bordered with white and emblazoned with mullets or five-pointed stars, corresponding in number to that of the Confederate States; the field to be white, except the outer half from the union to be a red bar extending the width of the flag.' According to Rogers, the white symbolized purity and innocence, and the red fortitude and courage. The cross of St. Andrew indicated descent from British stock, while the red bar was taken from the French flag, as

This Second National Flag was used as the headquarters flag of Maj. Gen. Robert F. Hoke, who commanded troops defending Petersburg, Virginia, until ordered in December 1864, to North Carolina, where he served until surrendering with Joseph Johnston's army after Bentonville. (North Carolina Museum of History)

This machine-sewn Second National Flag is the product of the Richmond Clothing Depot and bears the unit designation around the centre star in the canton along with battle honours, the latest of which is Gettysburg (1–3 July 1863). (North Carolina Museum of History)

many other Southerners were descended from French stock.

After a great deal of consideration the bill was passed by the Senate without change on 6 February 1865 and by the House of Representatives on 27 February. It was signed into law on 4 March 1865 — at which time the Confederacy measured its continued political existence in weeks. Indeed, because the Confederacy was so short-lived, few Third National Flags were made and most of those that were, were made by simply shortening the fly of Second National Flags and adding the red bar.

BATTLE FLAGS

The Army of Northern Virginia

As indicated above, the first major battle of the war, Bull Run or First Manassas, brought to light problems in using the First National Flag on the field of combat. For example, then-brigade commander Jubal Early was advised at one point during the battle that his regiments were firing on friends. Although he thought it was not so, he halted his men and rode out to where he could see a regiment drawn in battle line several hundred yards away. 'The dress of the volunteers on both sides at that time was very similar,' he later wrote, 'and the flag of the regiment I saw was drooping around the staff, so that I could not see whether it was the United States or Confederate flag.' It was not until the regiment in question fell back that he 'saw the United States flag unfurled and discovered the mistake'. In the meantime, precious time had been lost.

After this problem became evident the commander of the army in northern Virginia, Gen. Joseph E. Johnston, ordered that his regiments carry their state

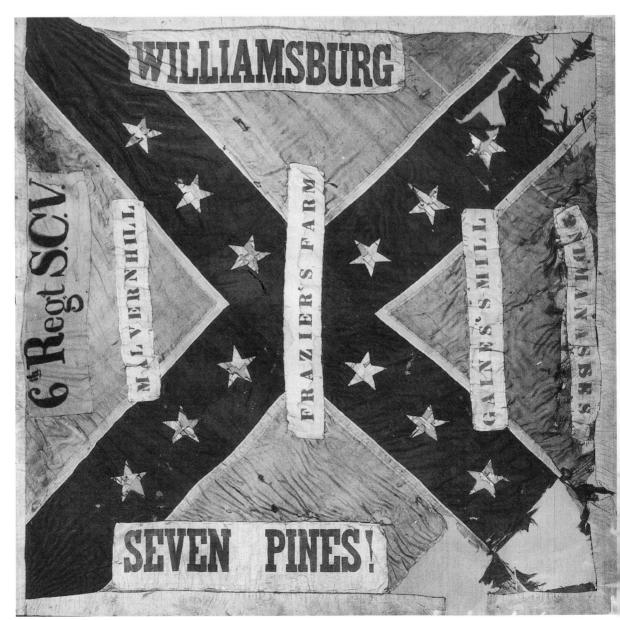

flags. Only Virginia regiments were able to obtain enough state flags for this purpose. Moreover, some state flags were too similar to colours carried by Union forces. The dark blue field of the Virginia state flag, for example, when lying limp, would look exactly like that of the US Army infantry regimental colour, which also featured a dark blue field.

To solve this problem, Congressman William Porcher Miles suggested to Gen. Beauregard that the army adopt as a battle flag the pattern which he had designed for the First National Flag—a pattern which Congress had rejected twice. On 27 August 1861 Miles sent Beauregard a drawing of his suggested flag, adding that his design called for, '... the ground Red, the Cross Blue (edged with white), Stars, White. This was my favorite. The three colours of Red, White, and Blue were preserved in it. It avoided the religous objection about the cross ...

it being the "Saltire" of Heraldry and significant of strength and progress ... The Stars ought always to be White or Argent because they are then blazoned "Proper" (or natural colour). Stars too show better on an Azure field than any other. Blue Stars on a White field would not be handsome or appropriate. The "White edge" (as I term it) to the Blue is partly a necessity to prevent what is called "false blazonry"... It would not do to put a blue cross therefore on a red field ... The introduction of the white between the Blue and Red adds also much to the brilliancy of the colours and brings them out in strong relief.'

Beauregard liked the design, writing to Miles on 4 September 1861: 'I regret to hear of the failure about the change of flag; but what can now be done is, to authorize commanding generals in the field to furnish their troops with a "field, or battle flag," which shall be according to your design, leaving out,

This first pattern Army of Northern Virginia battle flag was carried by the 6th South Carolina Infantry. The large block battle honours were the first style produced and were issued to Longstreet's troops. (South Carolina Confederate Relic Room and Museum)

The Army of Northern Virginia battle flag carried by the 16th Regiment, North Carolina State Troops. (North Carolina Department of Archives and History)

three Richmond belles, Hettie, Jennie, and Constance Cary. According to Constance, 'They were jaunty squares of scarlet crossed with dark blue edged with white, the cross bearing stars to indicate the number of the seceded States. We set our best stitches upon them, edged them with golden fringes, and, when they were finished, dispatched one to Johnston, another to Beauregard, and the third to Earl Van Dorn, then commanding infantry at Manassas. The banners were received with all possible enthusiasm; were toasted, feted, and cheered abundantly.'

The original flag sent to Van Dorn survives in the collection of the Museum of the Confederacy, Richmond, Virginia. It has a red field with a blue St. Andrew's cross with white fimbration and hoist edge, with three white ties to hold it to the staff. Three gold stars are set on each arm of the cross, clustered close to the centre; there is no star where the arms of the cross meet. It has 3-inch-long yellow fringing, and is actually 31 inches by 30 inches in size rather than perfectly square. The name 'Constance' has been embroidered on the lower arm of the cross near the hoist.

Three sizes were established for the battle flags made to this design and finally issued throughout the Army of Northern Virginia. Infantry versions were to be 48 inches on each side; artillery versions, 36 inches square; and cavalry versions, 30 inches square.

The first pattern Army of Northern Virginia battle flags were made as the samples were, sewn of dress silk by Richmond ladies under contract. Their blue crosses were eight inches wide, edged with $\frac{3}{4}$-inch-wide white silk. The 12 white stars were $4\frac{1}{2}$ inches in diameter, set 8 inches apart from the centre of the cross. All the edges but the hoist were bound in yellow silk; the hoist had a blue silk sleeve. Finally, the fields tended to be pinkish rather than scarlet.

Not all of these flags were made by official contractors from the start. The 4th Texas Infantry, for example, received in November 1861 a variant of this flag which was made by Miss Lula Wigfall, daughter of one of Texas' senators. This 47-inch-square silk flag was very similar to the first pattern except that it featured a single star at the point where the arms of the cross met which was larger than the other stars—symbolic of the Lone Star of Texas. The other stars were placed rather towards the outer part

Emanuel Rudisill, Co. M, 16th North Carolina, was the regimental ensign. He wears the regulation state uniform in this post-war photograph which also shows the regimental

battle flag reproduced in the accompanying photograph. Note the axehead finial on the staff. (North Carolina Department of Archives and History)

however, the white border, or rim separating the blue from the red. I would have it simply a red ground with two blue bars crossing each other diagonally, on which shall be the white stars; a white or golden fringe might go all around the sides of the flag.'

Beauregard took the idea to Johnston, who also liked the basic design but changed its shape to square on the recommendation of the army's future quartermaster, who said that a square flag would save cloth. He also restored the white fimbration. Examples of the new battle flag were made in September 1861 by

of the arms of the cross, rather than being clustered towards the centre as on the first silk pattern flags. It was edged in yellow, with the edge on the hoist side folded around to make a sleeve for the staff. This battle-worn flag was retired to Texas for storage on 7 October 1862.

By that time, most of these colours had been worn out by much use in the field. However, in early 1862 the Richmond Clothing Depot had acquired sufficient stocks of bunting, both by purchase from England and by the capture of the US Navy Yard at Norfolk, Virginia. The Depot began manufacturing and issuing its own machine-sewn First Bunting Pattern, Army of Northern Virginia battle flags. These were very similar to the First Silk Pattern flags but made of bunting, with true scarlet fields. Instead of yellow silk edging they were made with orange flannel $1\frac{1}{2}$ inches wide; the orange rapidly became a somewhat dirty tan in colour after some time in the field. The thirteenth star was added at the centre of the cross, and the cotton stars were smaller, only 3 inches in diameter. They were set 6 inches apart from the centre of the cross. The fimbration was made of $\frac{1}{2}$- inch wide cotton. The staff side was made with a 2-inch-wide white canvas or linen heading with three whipped eyelets for ties.

These flags, often lacking any sort of designation such as battle honours or unit designation, quickly became the standard Army of Northern Virginia battle flag first issued to Longstreet's Right Wing in May 1862. One of these unmarked flags, for example, was carried by the 3rd Georgia Infantry throughout the war.

In the spring of 1862 the Depot slightly changed the colours it had been issuing. The blue cross was now made only $5\frac{1}{2}$ inches wide. The stars were also reduced in size, to $3\frac{3}{4}$ inches in diameter. The so-called Third Bunting Pattern flag appeared in late 1862, when the orange borders were replaced with white 2-inch-wide bunting.

The 16th North Carolina also carried this bunting pattern Army of Northern Virginia battle flag with the unit designation marked in yellow around the centre star. The flag carries US War Department capture number '57' on the lower hoist side. (North Carolina Museum of History)

BATTLE HONOURS

Generally it was First to Third Bunting Pattern battle flags which were seen by Col. Arthur Fremantle, Coldstream Guards, on a visit to the Army of Northern Virginia in late June 1863. 'The colours of the regiments differ from the blue battle flags I saw with Bragg's Army (The Army of Tennessee),' he wrote. 'They are generally red, with a blue St. Andrew's cross showing the stars.... Most of the colours in this division (Pender's) bear the names Manassas, Fredericksburg, Seven Pines, Harpers Ferry, Chancellorsville, &c.'

These battle honours apparently first appeared in Longstreet's Corps in June 1862, with honours for Williamsburg and Seven Pines which had been printed on white strips and sewn to First Bunting Pattern battle flags (see Plate C2). Indeed, War Department General Orders No. 52, 23 July 1862, authorized placing on the battle flag the name of every battle in which the 'regiments, battalions, and separate squadrons have been actually engaged'.

There was no regulation method of applying battle honours; the first ones were usually sewn to the top and bottom, but also to the sides and the centre. Other units painted or embroidered battle honours on their colours; indeed, Richmond Clothing Depot flags supplied with the unit designations in yellow around the centre star bore battle honours painted by Depot workers.

Wisconsin Col. Frank Haskell, who saw the 'red flags wave' at Pickett's Charge at Gettysburg, afterwards found captured Confederate battle flags 'inscribed with "First Manassas," the numerous battles of the Peninsula, "Second Manassas," "South Mountain," "Sharpsburg," (our Antietam) "Fredericksburg," "Chancellorsville," and many more names.'

It should be noted, however, that most Army of Northern Virginia battle flags were apparently not marked with any sort of either unit designation or battle honours, even though in some commands marking the battle flags was regulation so that there could be no 'misunderstanding' over lost flags.

A new pattern Army of Northern Virginia battle flag was introduced in the spring of 1864 by the Depot. It was almost 51 inches square, with 7-inch-

The 22nd North Carolina carried this battle flag, which is virtually identical to that carried by the 16th North Carolina. (North Carolina Museum of History)

wide blue crosses and $\frac{5}{8}$-inch wide fimbration. The stars were $5\frac{1}{2}$ inches in diameter, placed 8 inches apart from the centre stars in a staggered orientation.

Apparently to conserve fabric, the Depot reverted to the original sized colours in November 1864. The cross was made 5 inches wide, but the stars were now $4\frac{1}{2}$ inches in diameter and 9 inches from each other. In the winter the Depot began placing the stars only 8 inches apart; and in March 1865 it changed the pattern to leave 7-inch intervals between them. All told, between 1862 and 1865 there were eight variations of the Army of Northern Virginia battle flag manufactured officially and issued to its regiments. Moreover, since its initial proponents, Beauregard and Johnston, went on to serve in many other theatres, its design formed the basis for most other armies' and departments' issue colours.

Yet these were not the only flags carried in the Army of Northern Virginia. Various national and state flags were used by some units. Some headquarters also used other types of flags, especially, as noted, various national flags. The army's engineering headquarters was marked by a large all-red bunting flag bearing the letters 'Chief Engineer.' on the top line and 'A.N.V.' on the bottom line, all in crude 11-inch white letters; the flag itself measures 3 feet $8\frac{1}{2}$ inches by 5 feet 9 inches.

The Army of Tennessee

The major army defending the heartland of the Confederacy, the line from the Mississippi River to Virginia, was the Army of Tennessee. Its leaders, too, found that the First National Flag was too similar to that flown by US troops and switched to new battle flag patterns. Instead, however, of one army-wide colour being regulation, each army corps carried colours of its commander's choosing. By 1863 these colours were fairly uniform within each corps, although this uniformity did not extend to the materials from which they were made until 1864.

Table B: Marked Army of Northern Virginia Battle Flags:

The units listed below, all but one of which are infantry regiments (the 1st Maryland was officially a battalion rather than a regiment) which served in the Army of Northern Virginia, are known to have carried second bunting pattern Army of Northern Virginia battle flags with the unit designation painted in yellow Roman uncial letters around the centre star, the number of the unit above the star and the two letter state designation below it (see Plates C4 and D4 for examples). Battle honours were painted in black Roman uncial letters on the field before the flags were issued. These flags were generally issued in September 1863.

Unit	ANV Brigades in which served	Unit	ANV Brigades in which served
14th Georgia	Hampton's, J. R. Anderson's, E. C. Thomas'	18th North Carolina	Branch's, Lane's
35th Georgia	Hampton's, J. R. Anderson's, E. C. Thomas'	23rd North Carolina	Early's, Garland's, Iverson's, R. D. Johnston's
45 Georgia	J. R. Anderson's, E. C. Thomas'		
49th Georgia	J. R. Anderson's, E. C. Thomas'	26th North Carolina	R. Ranson's, Pettigrew's, Kirkland's, MacRae's
10th Louisiana	McLaw's, Semmes', Starkes', Nicholl's, Iverson's, Strafford's, York's	28th North Carolina	Branch's, Lane's
1st Maryland Battalion	Elzy's	30th North Carolina	G. B. Anderson's, Ramseur's, Cox's
1st North Carolina	Ripley's, Colston's, Steuart's, Cox's		
2nd North Carolina	G. B. Anderson's, Ramseur's, Cox's	33rd North Carolina	Branch's, Lane's
4th North Carolina	Featherston's, G. B. Anderson's, Remseur's, Cox's	34th North Carolina	Pender's, Scales'
7th North Carolina	Branch's, Law's, Lane's	38th North Carolina	Pender's, Scales'
13th North Carolina	Colston's, Garland's, Pender's, Scales'	47th North Carolina	Pettigrew's, Kirkland's, MacRae's
16th North Carolina	W. Hampton's, Pender's, Scales'	Charlotte Artillery	Reserve artillery
		55th Virginia	Field's, H. H. Walker's, Barton's

Most of these early colours were made by H. Cassidy in New Orleans. In 1864 the job of supplying colours was taken on by the Atlanta and Selma, Georgia, Clothing Depots. James Cameron, of Mobile, Alabama, also made the colours under Quartermaster Department contract. Cameron also provided colours to the Army of Mississippi, which later became Polk's Corps of the Army of Tennessee.

The earliest Western battle flag appears to be that flown in Hardee's Corps of the Army of Tennessee. This was supposedly designed by Gen. Simon Bolivar Buckner for Gen. Albert Sidney Johnston's army in about September 1861. According to Buckner in later years, Johnston 'wanted a battle flag so distinctive in character that it could not be mistaken ... a blue field and a white centre.... My wife made such a flag for each regiment at Bowling Green.... The first time the battle flag was used was at Donelson. The troops that I commanded mostly fell to Hardee's command afterwards, they continued to use the flag, and it came to be known as Hardee's Battle Flag.'

'Each regiment carried a "battle flag,"' wrote Col. Fremantle after visiting Liddell's Brigade of Hardee's Corps, 'blue with a white border, on which were inscribed the names "Belmont," "Shiloh," "Perryville," "Richmond, Kentucky," and "Murfreesboro."' Hardee's Corps' battle flag was dark blue with a white border and a white oval or circle in its centre. The unit designation was often painted on the white disc, often called a 'silver moon', while battle honours were most often painted in dark blue on the border and sometimes in white on the field. At least one example exists, carried by an unknown unit, with the battle honour 'SHILOH' in dark blue on the white oval in the centre of the field.

Hardee's Corps battle flags were smaller than Army of Northern Virginia battle flags ranging from 31 to 34 inches on the hoist. They were often dyed with a poor quality blue dye and faded to a shade of pea-green after much use.

Regiments in the short-lived Army of Kentucky in the Department of East Tennessee, which were merged into the Army of Tennessee, apparently used a variation of the Hardee's Corps battle flag. It, too, had a blue field and white border but, instead of a disc, it had a white St. Andrew's Cross. Such a flag was described by Beauregard after the war, with the

The colour sergeant of the 12th Virginia Infantry Regiment, believed to be William C. Smith, holds the regiment's Army of Northern Virginia battle flag. This shows the size of the flag in comparison to a man. The flag also has cords and tassels, which have been coloured gold on the original print—cords were unusual among Confederate flags. (Lee A. Wallace, Jr., Collection)

The Army of Northern Virginia battle flag carried by the 24th Regiment, North Carolina State Troops, is all hand-sewn and has the unit designation stencilled on the upper border. Note US War Department capture number '275' marked on the upper border. (North Carolina Museum of History)

This unidentified Army of Northern Virginia battle flag, one of the last bunting types produced, was captured at the Battle of Saylor's Creek, Virginia, on 6 April 1865. (Museum of the Confederacy)

addition of 'blue or gold stars', as having been in Polk's command. A surviving example, without stars, was carried by the 30th Arkansas Infantry until it was captured on 31 December 1862. It measures 40 inches on the hoist by 46 inches, with white letters outlined in black on the top border '30th REG' and 'ARK INF' on the bottom border. The flag also had white outlined battle honours for 'FARMINGTON/MISS' on the top field and 'RICHMOND/KY' on the bottom field.

The colour adopted in Polk's Corps possibly draws its inspiration from Polk's pre-war service as an Episcopal bishop. Adopted in March 1862, it featured the cross of St. George, the emblem of the Episcopal Church, on a dark blue field. Typically, with these battle flags the cross of St. George was red, edged in white, with 11 five-pointed white stars. However, battle flags from Alabama regiments, including the 22nd and 24th Alabama Infantry from Withers' Division, lacked the red cross and stars. These battle flags, too, came in a wide variety of sizes, that of e.g. the 1st Tennessee Infantry being only 28 inches on the hoist, while that of the 22nd Alabama is $41\frac{1}{2}$ inches on the hoist.

On 23 November 1862 Maj. Gen. Benjamin F. Cheatham authorized the placing of a pair of crossed cannon on the battle flag of any regiment in his division of Polk's Corps that had overrun and captured Union artillery in action. A month later this order was made army-wide. These cannon appear in both dark blue on a white field and white on a dark blue or red field; the muzzles usually point down—indeed, they are often noted as being 'inverted'—but they sometimes point up.

Bragg's Corps was added to the Army of Tennessee in February 1862. At that time regiments in the corps, which had no uniform type of battle flag, were issued battle flags very similar to the first Army of Northern Virginia pattern. Since Beauregard designed the flags the similarity between these and the Army of Northern Virginia battle flags comes as no surprise. The Bragg's Corps models were, however, made of bunting instead of silk, with a broad pink border and 12 six-pointed, rather than five-pointed, stars. One of these battle flags, carried by the 7th Mississippi Infantry, measures $48\frac{1}{2}$ inches on the hoist and $42\frac{1}{2}$ on the fly.

Several months after the first shipment of Bragg's Corps battle flags appeared a second issue was made. These flags differed from the first issue in being rectangular instead of virtually square. An original carried by the 57th Georgia Infantry measures $42\frac{1}{2}$

1: First National Flag
2: Co. E, 1st Kentucky Infantry Regiment
3: Co. D, 21st Mississippi Infantry Regiment

A

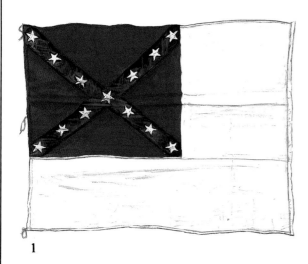

1

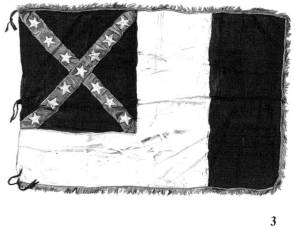

3

2

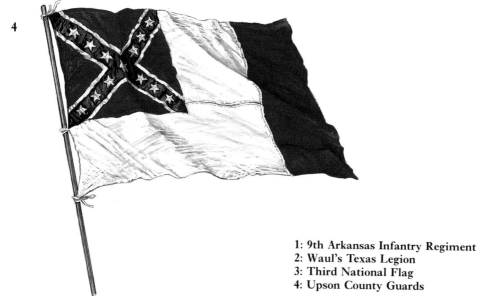

4

1: 9th Arkansas Infantry Regiment
2: Waul's Texas Legion
3: Third National Flag
4: Upson County Guards

B

1

2

3

4

1: 8th Virginia Infantry Regiment
2: 4th North Carolina Infantry Regiment
3: 5th Florida Infantry Regiment
4: 49th Georgia Infantry Regiment

C

1

3

2

4

1: 7th Virginia Infantry Regiment
2: 28th North Carolina Infantry Regiment
3: 9th Virginia Infantry Regiment
4: Co. C, 10th North Carolina Regiment Volunteers – 1st Artillery

D

1

2

3

4

1: 4th Missouri Infantry Regiment
2: 15th Arkansas Infantry Regiment
3: 1st Missouri Cavalry Regiment
4: 3rd Kentucky Mounted Infantry Regiment

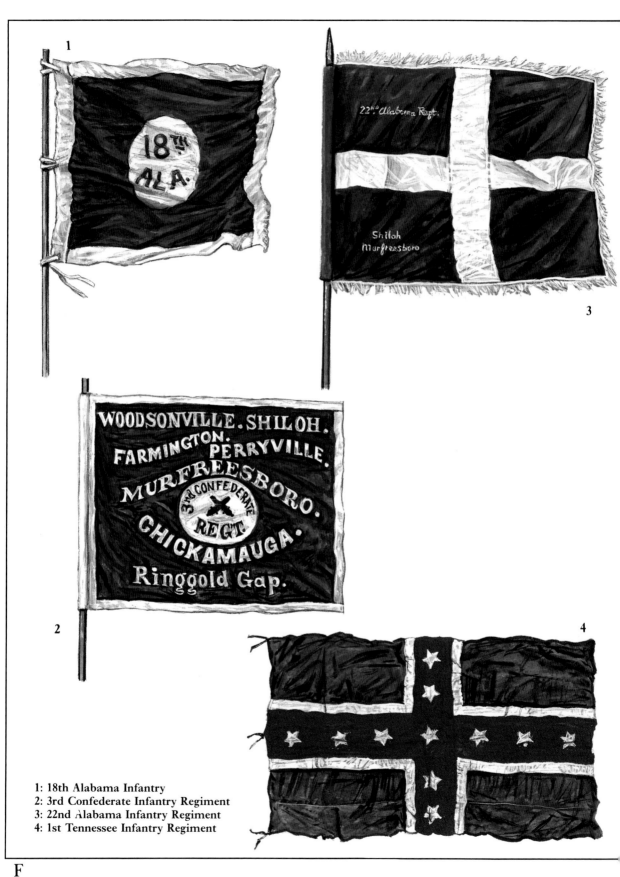

1: 18th Alabama Infantry
2: 3rd Confederate Infantry Regiment
3: 22nd Alabama Infantry Regiment
4: 1st Tennessee Infantry Regiment

F

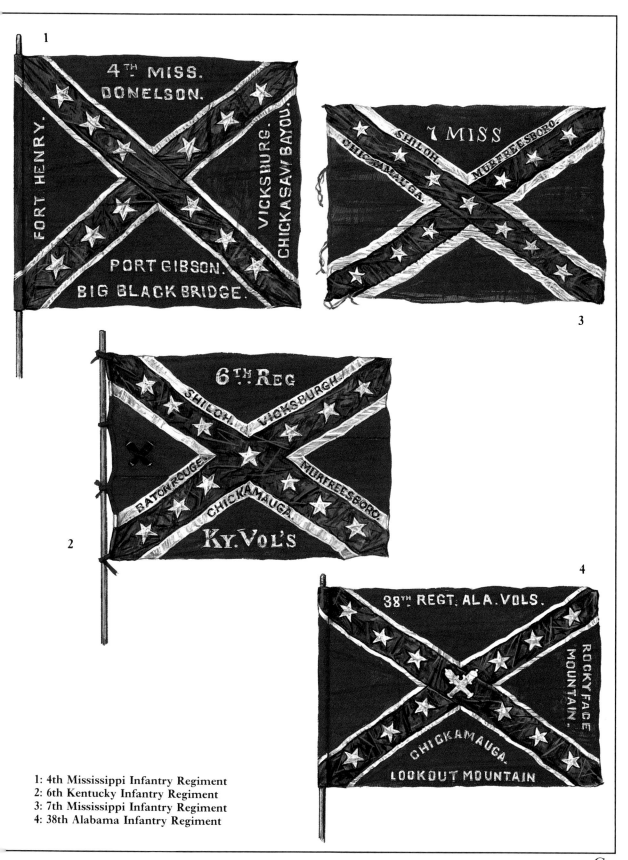

1: 4th Mississippi Infantry Regiment
2: 6th Kentucky Infantry Regiment
3: 7th Mississippi Infantry Regiment
4: 38th Alabama Infantry Regiment

G

1: 57th Georgia Infantry Regiment
2: 26th South Carolina Infantry
3: Shea's Vernon's Texas Battery

H

inches on the hoist by $73\frac{1}{2}$ inches on the fly. Moreover, the rectangular battle flags were edged with a pink border on all four sides, with a narrow white bunting border on the hoist through which nine holes were provided for flies to attach the flag to the staff.

Regiments of the Army of Tennessee's Reserve Corps, commanded by Gen. John C. Breckinridge, carried the First National Flag.

In December 1863 Gen. Joseph Johnston assumed command of the Army of Tennessee and issued orders to replace the hodge-podge of battle flags with a single army-wide model. The selected pattern was that of the Army of Northern Virginia, but the new regulation colours were to be rectangular, lacking a border, some three feet on the hoist by four and a quarter feet on the fly for infantry and cavalry, and two and a half on the hoist by three and a third on the fly for artillery batteries. These new battle flags were issued throughout March and April. They became known as the 'Army of Tennessee

battle flag' or the 'Johnston battle flag'. Most 'Confederate flags' flown today are of this pattern.

The officers and men of Maj. Gen. Patrick Cleburne's Division of Hardee's Corps strongly objected to losing their prized battle flags. Their feelings were heeded; and Cleburne's Division, to the end, continued to carry their unique battle flags while most of the rest carried the Army of Tennessee pattern. After the war Hardee wrote: 'This was the only division in the Confederate service to carry in action other than the national colors: and friends and foes soon learned to watch the course of the blue flag that marked where Cleburne was in battle.'

A hero of the Army of Northern Virginia, Lt. Gen. John Hood, was given command of one of the

This Army of Tennessee or 'Johnston' battle flag was carried by the 39th North Carolina State Troops. The unit designation and battle honours have been *applied with white cotton letters and numbers. The black capture number '456' is stamped in the upper field. (North Carolina Museum of History)*

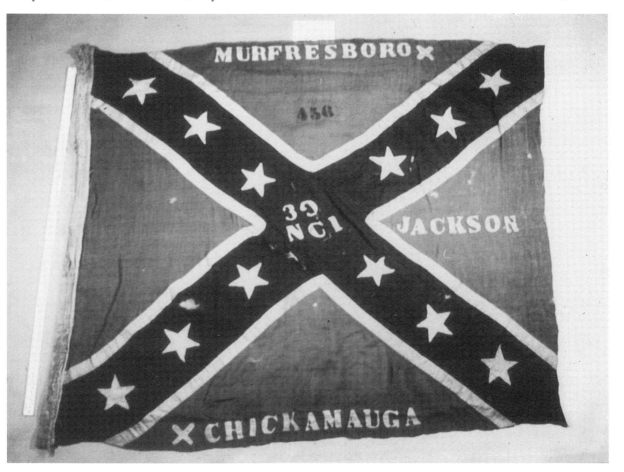

Table C: Army of Tennessee, Hardee's Corps Flags

The following representative variations of Hardee's Corps flags are known. The differences in the ways the unit designation and battle honours have been applied give some idea of the latitude granted unit commanders to alter even regulation corps flags within the Army of Tennessee. If the honours were on the border, they were in dark blue; if on the field, they were white.

18th Ala Inf	18th ALA. in disc, otherwise plain	4th Ky Inf	4th Ky in disc; SHILOH . VICKSBURG 1862 on top border; BATON ROUGE on fly border; MURFREESBORO . CHICKAMAUGA on bottom border
8th Ark Inf	8th ARKS in disc; PERRYVILLE on top border; SHILOH on hoist border; MURFREESBORO on fly border		
8th & 19th Ark Inf (combined)	8th & 19th Ark. Regts. over crossed cannon in disc; ARK. in white letters on left of disc in white, battle honours SHILOH, ELK HORN, Perryville, MURFREESBORO, Post Liberty, Chickamauga, TUNNEL HILL TENN., Ringgold Gap on Field	17th Tenn Inf	17th Tenn REG'T around crossed cannon in disc; PERRYVILLE on top border; MURFREESBORO on bottom border
		Swett's Btry	Battery name and crossed cannon in disc, battle honours SHILOH, MURFREESBORO, CHICKAMAUGA, TUNNEL HILL on blue field,
3rd CS Inf	3rd CONFEDERATE REG'T around crossed cannon in disc; battle honours WOODSONVILLE. SHILOH. FARMINGTON. PERRYVILLE. MURFREESBORO. CHICKAMAUGA. Ringgold Gap. on field	Unknown	Plain with battle honour SHILOH in disc
		Unknown	Plain (captured 24 Noveber 1863)

The 1st Virginia Cavalry were sketched in late August 1862 in Maryland just before the Battle of Sharpsburg carrying a small Army of Northern Virginia battle flag as a pennon.

The flag carried by Morton's Battery, which served with Forrest's command in the West, is a variation of the Army of Northern Virginia battle flag made without fimbration. Measuring 18 inches by 24 inches, it is made of cotton save for the St. Andrew's cross which is made of satin from the dress worn by the battery commander's wife on the day that the two met. Several stars are missing. (Courtesy Mike Miner)

army's corps on 1 February 1864. On 20 April he issued his corps' General Orders No. 54: 'I. The regiments of this corps will have their battle-flags plainly marked with their numbers and the State to which they belong. This is done that in the event of the loss of colors no misunderstanding may arise as to who lost them.

'II. But one stand of colors will be used by any regiment in time of battle.'

On 21 April 1864 a circular directed that units which had served honourably in battle or captured enemy artillery could inscribe the battle name on their battle flags. On that same day a circular was issued in Hardee's Corps which read: 'The battle-flags of this corps, known as the "Virginia battle-flag," will have inscribed on them the number of the regiment and the State to which it belongs; the number in the upper angle formed by the cross and the name of the State in the lower angle.'

Actually, there was some variety among flags even after the Army of Tennessee pattern battle flag was adopted; e.g. the 5th Company of Louisiana's Washington Light Artillery received a Second National Flag in early 1864 which had a red crossed cannon insignia on the white field over the name '5TH CO. W.A.' and six battle honours. Similar flags were carried by the 32nd Alabama Infantry and Austin's Battalion.

In an attempt to further regularize flags within the Army of Tennessee, on 19 February 1864 General Orders No. 25 authorized a system of command flags. They were as follows:

Army Headquarters: 'battle flag of the Virginia army.'

Hardee's Corps:

Corps commander: flag with three horizontal bars, blue-white-blue.

Division commanders: flag with two horizontal bars, white above blue.

Brigadiers: all blue flag.

Hindman's Corps: same, with red instead of blue.

OTHER COMMANDS

South Carolina, Georgia, and Florida

On 29 August 1862 Beauregard was named to command the Department of South Carolina and Georgia, which was expanded with the addition of the state of Florida on 7 October. At its strongest, in January 1864, some 38,277 officers and men were on department rolls. Until Beauregard arrived there units within the department, which was charged with

Field grade officers pose in front of an Army of Tennessee or 'Johnston' version of the Army of Northern Virginia battle flag carried by the 27th Texas Cavalry Regiment. The flag is very much the same as that carried by the 3rd Texas Cavalry, also a unit of Ross's Brigade which served in the Army of Tennessee until the 1864 Tennessee campaign. (Houston Public Library)

coastal defence, had flown a mixture of First National and state flags.

Shortly after assuming command, in September, Beauregard issued orders for a common design for standards and colours; however, it took some time for all the units within the department to receive the new flags. For example, it was not until late April 1863 that Beauregard presented units on James Island, South Carolina, with their new battle flags—flags which were received, according to one eyewitness, with 'three cheers and a Tiger'.

The new flag was basically the Army of Northern Virginia battle flag (see Plate H2), with some basic differences. The department flag was made in only two sizes: infantry, foot artillery, and cavalry had colours four feet square, while light artillery batteries flew three-foot-square standards. These flags also had bunting sleeves which were blue for infantry and red for both artillery and cavalry. Finally, the stars in the St. Andrew's cross were spaced evenly, rather than bunched towards the centre star as they were on Army of Northern Virginia battle flags.

The department's flags were made by both Quartermaster Clothing Depots within its domain; and by a private contractor, Hayden & Whilden, which was located in Charleston, South Carolina, where department headquarters was located until October 1864 when its new commander, Hardee, moved it to Savannah, Georgia, in preparation for the siege of that city.

Department General Orders No. 35 dated 5 April 1865 ordered that ambulance depots be marked with a plain red flag so that they would be easily visible by wounded and stretcher bearers.

Alabama, Mississippi, and East Louisiana

This department was created 9 May 1864 under the command of Maj. Gen. Stephen D. Lee. He was replaced in late July by Maj. Gen. Dabney H. Maury, who was in turn replaced by Lt. Gen. Richard Taylor, who held the command until the war's end. The department's headquarters was at Meridian, Mississippi, and had some 35,676 officers and men on paper; only 12,000 were surrendered in May 1865.

Units within the department had flown a mixture of national flags, flags patterned on Army of Northern Virginia battle flags, and state flags. However, shortly after the department was created a standard pattern for its battle flag was adopted and examples were made at Mobile, Alabama, and issued to units within it.

The wool bunting flags were rectangular copies of the Army of Northern Virginia battle flag made with a dozen white stars, three on each arm of the St. Andrew's cross and none in its centre (see Plate G1). Second National Flags made at Mobile also lack this centre star within their cantons. The flags were made without borders and with a leading edge sewn around to make a pole sleeve. Most examples measure around 45 inches on the hoist by 52 inches. A cavalry standard some 37 inches on the hoist by 46 inches was issued to regiments within Lt. Gen. Nathan Bedford Forrest's cavalry corps.

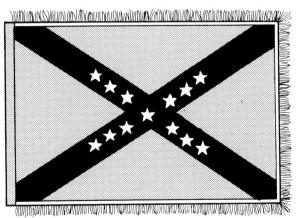

The 28th Alabama Infantry, which served in the Army of Tennessee, carried this novel battle flag. The obverse was a variation of the Army of Northern Virginia battle flag with a dark blue St. Andrew's cross and gold stars, while the reverse was of white silk bearing the design and lettering in gold. The fringe was also gold.

PERRYVILE

17th Tenn X REGt

MURFREESBORO

This 'Hardee's pattern' battle flag was carried by the 17th Tennessee, which was merged with the 23rd *Tennessee after the battles of Murfreesboro and Chickamauga.*

Trans-Mississippi Department

Initially there was little in the way of unified design or effort to provide standardized flags within the Confederate state west of the Mississippi River. On 18 November 1861 the Chief Quartermaster, Department of Texas, bought '3 large Flags,' made from 68 yards of bunting, from Samuel Maas, but this seems to have been the only centralized purchase or manufacture of flags within the area. State flags were quite common, especially in the war's early years.

On 19 April 1864 the department's headquarters issued its General Orders No. 18 which authorized battle honours on flags within the command area.

Van Dorn's Corps

On 19 September 1861 Earl Van Dorn was commissioned a major-general in the Confederate Army and assigned to Virginia. There he was one of three commanders to receive a sample of what became the basic Army of Northern Virginia battle flag. However, when he was assigned as commander of the Army of the West in the Trans-Mississippi theatre in January 1862 he came up with an entirely different design of battle flag which he had his men fly.

On 7 February 1862 Van Dorn wrote to one of his subordinates, Brig. Gen. Sterling Price: 'So many mistakes have occurred during this war by the similarity of flags that I have had a battle-flag made, one of which I send you for your army. Please have one made for each regiment of your army, to be carried in battle.'

His flag was of a plain red field with 13 white five-pointed stars placed in various arrangements of five or three rows (see Plates E1 and E2). A white crescent, which supposedly represents Missouri, was placed in the upper left corner. A yellow fringe was sometimes sewn directly to the red field and sometimes around a white border. When first used they were plain, but battle honours and unit designations were apparently added later. The original Van Dorn flag of the 15th Arkansas Infantry measures 46 inches by 65 inches, and is made of bunting.

In April 1862 Van Dorn's men were assigned to the Army of the Mississippi as Van Dorn's Corps. On 17 July 1862 all the regiments of the Army of the Mississippi were authorized to have a battle honour for Shiloh inscribed on their battle flags; on 11 June orders issued in Maury's Division read, 'For conspicuous gallantry in the battle of Shiloh, the Second Texas Regiment will have Shiloh enscribed on its battle flag.' A similar battle honour was authorized for Murfreesboro. There were no regulation methods of applying these honours; some were sewn on from separate letters, some painted, and some embroidered.

These colours continued to be used thereafter, being carried at the Battle of Corinth in October 1862. Examples were being made and issued new as late as the fall of 1862, and these lasted until the surrender of Vicksburg, 4 July 1863. Thereafter this particular flag design seems to have passed into disuse.

District of Western Louisiana

In early 1864 troops of Lt. Gen. Richard Taylor's command, which had cleared out Western Louisiana, appear to have carried uniform flags. These were similar to the last pattern flag carried in the Army of Tennessee save that the colours were reversed, with dark blue fields and red St. Andrew's crosses. Stars and fimbration were white.

An original flag of this type was carried by the 3rd Texas Infantry. It has a yellow fringe, and a white unit designation embroidered on the field: THIRD is embroidered in the top triangle of the field, REGT in the hoist triangle, TEXAS in the fly triangle, and INFANTRY in the bottom triangle. It measures 45 by 48½ inches.

The flag of the 2nd Louisiana Cavalry was similar, differing in that it lacked the white fimbration and was edged in gold braid border. The unit designation was also embroidered, but in buff script, with '2nd La.' in the upper triangle and 'Cavalry.' in the lower one.

The 1st Arkansas Cavalry carried a variation of this flag, with a St. George's cross instead of a St. Andrew's cross.

Other Trans-Mississippi flags

Although there was a wide variety of flags flown in the command, and a real lack of hard information about them, there do seem to have been several distinctive battle flags within the command by 1863.

On 31 May 1862 the 6th Texas Infantry Regiment, which had been organized in mid-1861, received a regimental colour. According to the *Galveston Advocate* of that date, 'We have had the gratification of seeing the flag prepared for Col. [Robert S.] Garland's regiment, by Mrs. R. Owens and her daughters of this place. It is a beautiful thing indeed. The material is of the richest kind, the work on its exquisite and the designs in good taste – the ground red, the border white, a shield of blue in the center. It contains twelve stars in a circle made of white silk or satin, with one large Texas star in the center. But a few regiments march under a more beautiful flag, and but few flags wave over a more valiant regiment. May the Guardian Power protect the regiment and the flag.'

Mrs. Owens herself later wrote: 'The flag was made of red merino, somewhat larger than the ordinary regimental flag, with a border of white silk fringe. There was a blue shield, 28 by 36 inches, which contained 13 stars. Of these stars 12 were arranged along the margin of the shield, six on either side, while the center star was larger than the others and intended to indicate the Lone Star State. Neatly stitched in white silk were the words "Sixth Texas Infantry Regiment."'

A somewhat similar flag was supposedly carried by the 17th Texas Infantry. It had a red cotton field with a narrow white silk border on top, bottom, and fly, with the staff edge folded over to make a sleeve for

This 'Hardee's pattern' battle flag, carried by an unidentified unit, has been dated to the spring of 1863. The original is in a private collection.

the staff. A somewhat elliptical blue cotton circle was placed half way between the top and bottom of the field, close to the staff. This 9¼ inch by 10 inch diameter disc had a dozen white cotton flannel stars in a circle around its edge with a single larger star in its centre. The motto TRUST IN GOD was embroidered in white Roman uncial letters along the bottom of the flag. The similarity of the 6th and 17th Texas Infantry regimental flags suggests that this was a somewhat standard pattern in the area.

Two other very similar flags from the Trans-Mississippi Department also exist. Both have red fields with dark blue St. Andrew's crosses without white fimbration, but with a white star at the point where the cross arms meet, and three stars near that point but in the field rather than on the arms of the cross. One was captured by the 15th Maine Infantry while it was in Texas. The other is marked with block letters on the arm of the cross from upper left to lower right ROBERTSON CAVLILERS! (sic) and on the other arm of the cross GOD FOR THE RIGHT! It was apparently captured by an Illinois unit in the West. While the first flag had a plain border, the second had a yellow silk fringe.

A similar battle flag which lacked either unit designation or stars was captured from either the 18th

Louisiana Infantry, the 24th Louisiana Infantry, or Battery H, 1st Mississippi Light Infantry on 27 October 1862 in Eastern Louisiana. It has been suggested that the flag probably belonged to the artillery battery, since the two infantry regiments had recently been transferred from Bragg's Corps of the Army of the Mississippi which had recently received Army of Northern Virginia pattern battle flags. This also suggests that the flag's style was one used in the District of Eastern Louisiana.

Confederate Missouri regiments often carried a flag that was apparently unique to units from that state, although it was not an official state flag. It had a dark blue field, bordered in red on top, bottom, and fly, with a white Roman cross placed near the hoist. The hoist end of the flag was simply folded over to make a sleeve for the staff. An example of these was carried by the 1st Missouri Cavalry (see Plate E3).

Indian Commands

The Confederacy recruited widely in the Indian Territories, now Oklahoma, for all-Indian units. These included eight mounted units—cavalry or mounted rifle regiments or battalions—and three infantry regiments. These units were organized along tribal lines.

The Cherokee Nation received its own flag from Confederate Indian Commissioner Albert Pike on 7 October 1861. It was a First National Flag with the Roman uncial letters 'CHEROKEE BRAVES' painted in red on the white stripe. The cotton flag measures 49 inches by 79 inches. The canton contains the standard 11 white five-pointed stars, each representing a Confederate state, in a circle; but within the circle is a smaller circle of four red five-pointed stars around a single, slightly larger red five-pointed star. These stars stood for the Five Civilized Tribes of the Cherokee, Seminole, Chickasaw, Creek, and Choctaw. This flag was carried by the 1st Cherokee Mounted Rifles and was captured on 3 July 1862. Another version was virtually identical, but eliminated the star that represented the Seminoles.

The Choctaw Brigade, made up of some 2,000 Choctaw Indians, flew quite a different flag. It was 40 inches by 62 inches with a dark blue field. In its centre was a white circle surrounding a red disc, all of cotton. Embroidered on the red disc were a pair of crossed arrows, the points away from the hoist, with a tomahawk perpendicular to the ground and an unstrung bow facing the staff, all in white. The fact that the bow was unstrung was supposed to signify that the Choctaw were peace-loving, although ready to defend themselves.

OTHER FLAGS

There were no official pennons or guidons carried by Confederate troops. Officially, in the Army of Northern Virginia at least, regulation battle flags were simply made in small sizes for mounted units which carried such flags in the US Army.

However, a number of units did carry these small flags. For example, a forked guidon survived with its top half red and its bottom half white, marked in white on the top '1st Co. 1st Batl' and in red on the bottom 'N.C. ARTILLERY'. Many small forked guidons still exist, some 11 by 16 or 17 inches, made like the First National Flag. These were apparently made for use on lances.

Another pennon is supposed to have been taken from a 'lance staff' carried in the 5th Virginia Cavalry.

It measures 9¼ by 24 inches and has three horizontal stripes, the top and bottom red and the middle one white.

Apparently one Confederate battery carried a guidon made in the First National pattern, save that the stars in the canton are arranged in the pattern of a St. Andrew's cross. The rectangular pennon is 13 inches by 20 inches. A handwritten inscription on it indicates that it was captured in 1864.

Naval flags

Naval vessels fly three basic flags: the ensign, the jack, and the commission pennant. The ensign is the national flag and is flown at the ship's stern in most cases. The jack is flown only on a ship of war when in port, from the jack staff at the ship's bow; it designates the ship's nationality. The commission

pennant shows that the ship is in its country's service, and is flown from the mainmast.

The First National Flag served as the first naval ensign. Some versions were apparently made with the stars in rows rather than in a circle, although the latter was the most commonly seen canton.

The ensign was the ship's main symbol. Rear Admiral Raphael Semmes later recalled: 'At length on the 3rd of June [1861], I was enabled to put the *Sumter*, formally, in commission. On that day her colors were hoisted, for the first time—the ensign having been presented to me, by some patriotic ladies of New Orleans . . .'

A Hardee's Division battle flag captured from an unknown Confederate regiment on Lookout Mountain on 24 November 1863, and bearing the US War Department capture number '95'. (Museum of the Confederacy)

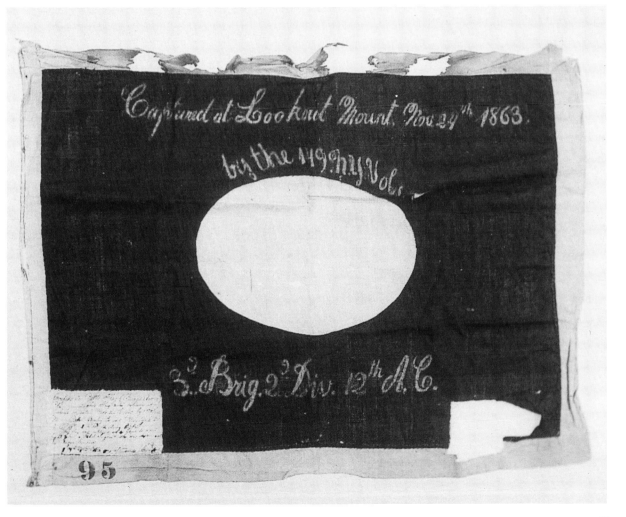

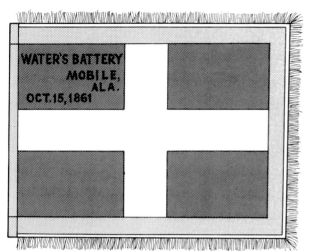

Apparently a variation of the East Tennessee battle flag, this example carried by Walter's Alabama Battery has a dark blue field with a white cross, red border and white fringe. The unit designation was embroidered in red.

As was typical of other English-speaking nations' navies, especially those of Britain and the United States, the canton of the First National Flag was used as the jack.

The design of the commission pennant is not known through orders, but an illustration in Semmes' memoirs indicates that it had a blue head with a white star representing each Confederate State, with three stripes, red, white, and red, the same as on the First National Flag.

To conform to the adoption of the Second National Flag the Secretary of the Navy issued regulations calling for new flags on 26 May 1863:

'The new Ensign will be made according to the following directions. The field to be white, the length one and a half times the width of the flag, with the union (now used as the Battle Flag) to be square, of two-thirds of the width of the flag, having the ground red, thereon a broad saltier of blue, to the union as 1:4⅘, bordered with white, to the union as 1:22, and emblazoned with white mullets, or five-pointed stars, diameter of the stars to the union as 1:6⅖ corresponding in number to that of the Confederate States.

'THE PENNANT. A white ground, its size to be as 1:72, or its length seventy-two times its width at the head, and tapering to a point.

'The union of the Pennant to be as follows: All red from the head for three times its width, with a white border equal to half its width, then all blue in length equal to twelve times its width, to be emblazoned with stars, in number equal to those in the Ensign, with a white border equal to half the width, and then red three times the width, with the fly all white.

'THE JACK. To be the same as the union for the Ensign, except that its length shall be one and a half times its width.'

A variation of the commission pennant is known to have had a St. Andrew's cross of blue, with white fimbration, on a red field, with the rest of the pennant in white. The arms of the cross lacked the regulation stars.

When the Third National Flag was adopted, as many ensigns as possible conforming to the new design would presumably have been issued. Given the few months left to the Confederate Navy, however, it is unlikely that very many, if any, were actually flown.

As well as a Navy, Confederate law provided for a Revenue Marine Customs Service. This was a small naval force provided with cutters in each major port, whose purpose was to make sure customs laws were enforced. Its command fell to the Secretary of the Treasury, rather than the Navy, although in wartime its cutters and officers and men could be taken into the Navy as needed. Although some US Revenue Marine Customs Service cutters were captured at the outbreak of the war and taken into Confederate service, few actually saw customs service. The

The First National Flag of the 20th Texas Infantry, which was stationed along the Texas coastline throughout the war, bears the unit motto and designation in gold-painted letters and numbers, edged on the upper right in red and the lower left in black.

blockade, which put an effective end to smuggling, also largely ended the need for customs enforcement.

Nonetheless, the service did have its own ensign. It looked rather like the French flag, with stripes of (from the staff of the fly) blue, white, and red. The blue stripe was one and a half times wider than the other stripes and had a circle of white five-pointed stars, one for each state, where the canton would be.

Select Bibliography

Cannon, Devereaux D., Jr., *The Flags of the Confederacy, An Illustrated History;* Memphis, Tennessee, 1988

Crute, Joseph H., Jr., *Emblems of Southern Valor;* Louisville, Kentucky, 1990

Madaus, H. Michael and Robert D. Needham, 'Unit Colors of the Trans-Mississippi Confederacy', *Military Collector & Historian;* Washington, DC, 1989

Madaus, H. Michael, *The Battle Flags of the Confederate Army of Tennessee;* Milwaukee, Wisconsin, 1976

Madaus, Howard M., 'The Conservation of Civil War Flags: The Military Historian's Perspective', *Papers presented at the Pennsylvania Capitol Preservation Committee Flag Symposium, 1987;* Harrisburg, 1987

Todd, Frederick P., *American Military Equippage, Vol. II;* Providence, Rhode Island, 1977

United Confederate Veterans, *The Flags of the Confederate States of America;* Baltimore, Maryland, 1907

The 3rd Louisiana Infantry received this battle flag after being reorganized after its surrender at Vicksburg in the summer of 1863. It served thereafter in the Trans-Mississippi Department under this flag. The battle honours and unit designation are applied with white cotton letters sewn onto the flag.

THE PLATES

A1: First National Flag

This variation of the First National Flag was captured from an unknown unit at Gettysburg. It is fairly typical of the First National Flag save that the stars are somewhat larger than usual. The infantry colour sergeant wears a first pattern Richmond Depot jacket, with the three stripes and a star officially designated for an ordnance sergeant but widely worn by colour sergeants.

A2: Co. E, 1st Kentucky Infantry Regiment

Companies were often presented with a colour on leaving for war. The unit designation was often placed on the white stripe in the field. This example of the First National Flag has an unusually sized canton, although six-pointed stars were not uncommon. The 1st Kentucky was formed in mid-1861 and served for one year in northern Virginia before disbandment.

A3: Co. D, 21st Mississippi Infantry Regiment

This First National Flag variation was made by the Woodville, Mississippi, Ladies' Auxiliary for the local Jefferson Davis Guards, which became Co. D, 21st Mississippi Infantry Regiment. The regiment served in the Army of Northern Virginia from the Seven Days' to Appomattox. The flag is made of wool with cotton stars; it is 49 inches on the hoist and 76 inches on the fly.

B1: 9th Arkansas Infantry Regiment

The canton of this Second National Flag is larger than regulation, and lacks the standard white fimbration. The 9th Arkansas surrendered at Port Hudson on 9 July 1863 and was paroled. After being exchanged it finished the war in the Army of

This red cotton flag was captured in Texas and is typical of a number of similar battle flags from that area. The St. Andrew's cross is dark blue and the cotton stars are white. Small holes along the hoist edge show where it was once nailed to a staff.

Tennessee, surrendering on 26 April 1865 in North Carolina.

B2: Waul's Texas Legion
This virtually regulation Second National Flag was made for Col. Bernard Timmons, who commanded the 12 infantry companies of Waul's Texas Legion. The colour was made when the unit was reformed after it was captured at Vicksburg in 1863. The unit served in the Trans-Mississippi Department until disbanded in May 1865.

B3: Third National Flag
This particular Third National Flag probably flew over some government installation. It lacks the regulation white fimbration, but is otherwise made according to the flag law of 4 March 1865.

B4: Upson County Guards
This Third National Flag was made in England in 1864 as a Second National Flag and had the red stripe at its end added later. It was captured from the Upson County, Georgia, Guards on 20 April 1865. Made of bunting and cotton, $42\frac{1}{2}$ inches at the hoist and $88\frac{1}{2}$ in the fly, it has a silk cross and stars.

C1: 8th Virginia Infantry Regiment
This first issue Army of Northern Virginia battle flag was supposedly made by the wife of Gen. Pierre G. T. Beauregard with silk from her own dresses, and presented to the 8th by the general in recognition of valour in the Battle of Balls Bluff. The 8th served in the Army of Northern Virginia until after Gettysburg, when it was transferred to the Department of Richmond which Beauregard commanded in 1864.

C2: 4th North Carolina Infantry Regiment
This first bunting issue Army of Northern Virginia battle flag bears battle honours printed on white cotton strips and sewn onto the colour. Identical honours were sewn on the battle flags of the 6th South Carolina and 2nd Florida Infantry Regiments (in the latter case they were sewn in the middle of the colour), among other regiments with the same style of battle honours. The regiments served in different divisions of Longstreet's Corps at the Seven Pines but were thereafter separated, so it is assumed that these honours were placed on the flags of units in that Corps shortly after the battle.

C3: 5th Florida Infantry Regiment
This first bunting pattern Army of Northern Virginia battle flag measures 47 inches square and was issued in early summer 1862. The 5th served in the Army of Northern Virginia from Second Manassas until it surrendered with only six officers and 47 enlisted men at Appomattox.

C4: 49th Georgia Infantry Regiment
Many of the third bunting pattern Army of Northern Virginia battle flags of regiments of the Army of Northern Virginia were made with the yellow painted unit designation as shown (see Table B). As seen by its battle honours, the regiment was an active one, until it surrendered with only eight officers and 103 enlisted men at Appomattox.

D1: 7th Virginia Infantry Regiment
The unit designation style on this third bunting pattern Army of Northern Virginia battle flag appears to have been common in Pickett's Division. While the 7th served in Kemper's and later W. R. Terry's brigades in that division, two other regiments with similar colours—the 18th and 28th Virginia Infantry Regiments—served in Garnett's and later Hunton's brigades in the same division. The flag of

the 18th has '18th Va.' embroidered in white on the hoist side of the field and 'Regt. Inf'y.' on the fly side of the hoist, as do those of the 7th and 28th Regiments.

D2: 28th North Carolina Infantry Regiment

This style of battle honours appears to have been unique to Lane's Brigade of A. P. Hill's Division of the Army of Northern Virginia, which included the 7th, 18th, 28th, 33rd, and 37th North Carolina Regiments. The surviving colour of the 37th North Carolina is identical to this one save that the honour at the top of the colour reads NEW BERNE, while that on the hoist is MALVERN HILL and that on the fly is MANNASSAS (sic).

D3: 9th Virginia Infantry Regiment

This rather crude unit designation on a third bunting pattern Army of Northern Virginia battle flag appears to have been executed within the unit. The 9th lost over half its officers and men at Gettysburg, surrendering with just two officers and 37 enlisted men at Appomattox.

D4: Co. C, 10th North Carolina Regiment Volunteers—1st Artillery

The 10th had five heavy and five light artillery companies, of which Co. C.—also known as the 'Charlotte Artillery'—was a light battery which served in the Army of Northern Virginia from July 1862. The type of unit designation shown here usually appears on third bunting pattern Army of Northern Virginia battle flags, as mentioned above.

E1: 4th Missouri Infantry Regiment

This is the Van Dorn pattern colour of the 4th Missouri, which was organized in April 1862 and was captured at Vicksburg in July 1863.

E2: 15th Arkansas Infantry Regiment

The 'NW' on this Van Dorn pattern colour represents the 15th's nickname, the 'Northwest Regiment'. The colour, 46 inches by 65 inches, was apparently presented to the unit in October or November 1862. One of three Arkansas units so numbered, this 15th was surrendered at Vicksburg and not reorganized thereafter.

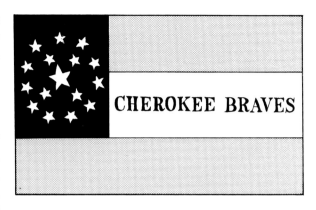

The First National Flag carried by the Cherokee Nation. The outer circle of stars are white and the inner circle red.

E3: 1st Missouri Cavalry Regiment

The 11th Wisconsin Infantry captured this Missouri pattern battle flag on 17 May 1863; it is 36 inches by 51 inches in size. The unit served from Elkhorn Tavern until it surrendered at Vicksburg. It was later exchanged, fighting at Atlanta and thereafter in Tennessee, finishing the war in the Department of Alabama, Mississippi, and East Louisiana.

E4: 3rd Kentucky Mounted Infantry Regiment

The 3rd was a part of Kentucky's 'Orphan Brigade' until late 1862 when it was reassigned. Nevertheless, it continued to fly this typical 'Orphan Brigade battle flag', a similar example of which indicated brigade headquarters. The unit was mounted in early 1864 and served in Mississippi, Georgia, and Alabama.

F1: 18th Alabama Infantry

The 18th, which served in the Army of Tennessee between March 1862 and January 1865, carried a typical Hardee's Corps battle flag which measured, in this case, 34 inches by $37\frac{1}{2}$ inches.

F2: 3rd Confederate Infantry Regiment

The 3rd was formed in January 1862 with troops from Arkansas and Mississippi. It was merged with the 5th Confederate Infantry from February 1863 until Aptil 1864, surrendering on 26 April 1865. Their Hardee's Corps battle flag measures 30 inches by $35\frac{1}{2}$ inches.

F3: 22nd Alabama Infantry Regiment

The 22nd's variation of the Polk's Corps battle flag was captured on 20 September 1863. The cotton flag is $41\frac{1}{2}$ inches by $54\frac{1}{2}$ inches, with a silk fringe. The unit designation and battle honours are embroidered. The 22nd lost 53 per cent of its officers and men killed or wounded at Chickamauga, also fighting at Franklin and Nashville.

F4: 1st Tennessee Infantry Regiment

The 1st carried a standard silk Polk's Corps battle flag measuring 28 inches by 46 inches. Later it had a black unit designation, '1st REGT TENN', painted on a white cotton strip sewn to the top centre of the flag. The 1st was consolidated with the 27th Tennessee in December 1862.

G1: 4th Mississippi Infantry Regiment

The 4th lost this Department of Alabama, Mississippi, and East Louisiana battle flag on 16 December 1864 at Nashville. It measures 46 inches by 52 inches.

G2: 6th Kentucky Infantry Regiment

The 6th, part of the 'Orphan Brigade', carried this Army of Tennessee pattern battle flag until it was captured on 1 September 1864. The battle honours and crossed cannon are painted on the bunting and cotton flag. This is $36\frac{1}{2}$ inches by 51 inches in size; the stars are 4 inches across at the points, while the unit designation letters are a maximum of 3 inches high. The crossed cannon are in honour of the capture of a Union battery at Chickamauga on the evening of 20 September 1863.

G3: 7th Mississippi Infantry Regiment

The 7th carried throughout the war a battle flag of the type used by the Army of Tennessee, in which it served after a brief tour of duty on the Mississippi coast. It surrendered with 74 officers and men on 26 April 1865.

G4: 38th Alabama Infantry Regiment

Typically inverted crossed cannon appear in the centre of this Army of Tennessee battle flag which was captured at Resaca, Georgia, on 15 May 1864. The 38th took 490 officers and men into battle at

The flag of the Choctaw Brigade has a blue field with a red disk fimbrated in white; the traditional Indian weapons are white.

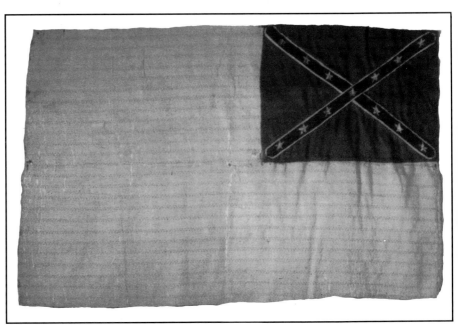

This Second National Flag is the naval jack flown on the CSS Shenandoah, *the last Confederate flag to be struck, which was finally lowered in November 1865 for the last time. The gold stars have been painted on the St. Andrew's cross. (North Carolina Museum of History)*

Chickamauga, and surrendered with only 80 on 4 May 1865.

H1: 57th Georgia Infantry Regiment

An ensign, bearing the insignia of a first lieutenant, was authorized in each regiment to carry the unit colour on 17 February 1864. This regiment's Army of Mississippi, Bragg's Corps battle flag, made of cotton with silk stars and border, measures $42\frac{1}{2}$ inches by $73\frac{1}{2}$ inches. The 57th was captured at Vicksburg, after which it was exchanged and served from Resaca to Bentonville.

H2: 26th South Carolina Infantry

The 26th served in Charleston, South Carolina, from late 1862 until early 1863, when it was sent to Mississippi; and then from mid-1863 until the spring of 1864 back in Charleston, before finally joining the Army of Northern Virginia at Petersburg. It must have received this Department of South Carolina, Georgia, and Florida battle flag during its latter tour of duty in Charleston.

H3: Shea's-Vernon's Texas Battery

This 36 inch by 46 inch silk flag, lacking the white fimbration and with a centre larger than the others, is typical of those carried by Texans who served in their own state and Louisiana. An almost identical standard was carried by Parson's Texas Cavalry Brigade.

UNION FLAGS

INTRODUCTION

The typical flag presentation ceremony of a national colour, here to a Kentucky regiment at Camp Bruce, near Cynthiana, Kentucky.

The regimental or battery set of colours was more than simply a unit designation, issued for the ease of a commander in identifying his units in the field. It was the very symbol of the regiment; it was its heart, the thing that drew its members together. As such it was fiercely defended in action, where it flew in the centre of the line, drawing enemy fire upon its carriers.

Each regiment received its colours in one of its first formal ceremonies, which itself was almost an initiation into the world of the soldier. On 12 November 1861 Pennsylvania's governor Andrew Curtin, accompanied by staff members, took the train from his capital city of Harrisburg to the county seat of Chester County to present a set of colours to the newly formed 97th Pennsylvania Volunteer Infantry Regiment. Arriving shortly after noon, the state officials were met by the entire regiment, which then escorted them to the city's court house. Following a speech introducing the governor and his return

speech to local citizens, the officials had dinner. Then, about three, they all met at the 97th's training camp located on the county fair grounds.

There, according to the regiment's historian: 'The Regiment was formed in column by division closed in mass in front of the stand, on the north side of the Fair buildings. The people had crowded around the reserved space with such eagerness as to render it difficult for the guard to clear sufficient room for the reception committee and those who were to take part in the proceedings.

'When all had been arranged, the Governor came forward, uncovered, holding the staff upon which waved the beautiful stars and stripes of the flag he was about to entrust to the keeping of the regiment, as its banner, around which to rally when led forth into the performance of whatever duty an imperiled country might demand, and, in these words consigned them

This national colour of the 2d Battalion, 18th US Infantry Regiment has its stars arranged in the canton in the manner of flags made by Evans and Hassall, Philadelphia. (West Point Museum Collection)

to the Regiment. . . .' Curtin spoke at great length, ending with this peroration:

'It is the flag of your fathers and your country. It will be yours to bear it in the thickest of the fight and to defend it to the last. Upon its return, it will have inscribed upon it the record of those battles through which you have carried it, and will become a part of the archives of Pennsylvania; and there it will remain, through all coming time, a witness to your children and your children's children of the valor of their fathers. With a full confidence that in your hands this banner will never be disgraced, I entrust it to your care and for the last time bid you farewell.'

In camp, the regimental colours flew over the unit headquarters as a guide post to members and outsiders alike. In combat, it was drawn into the very centre of action where, in obedience to millions of words like those spoken by Governor Curtin at thousands of presentations, it was fiercely defended. Take, for example, the 38th Pennsylvania Volunteer Infantry Regiment at Antietam. There the regiment

was one of dozens which stormed Confederate positions in the now famous Cornfield. According to the 1865 *History of the Pennyslvania Reserve Corps*, 'A most singular fatality fell upon the color bearers of this regiment. Sergeant Henry W. Blanchard, who had carried the regimental colors through all the storms of battle in which the regiment fought, was a most remarkable man. Born in Massachusetts in 1832, he was about thirty years old. He had the most complete control of his feelings; in the fiercest hours of battle, was always perfectly calm, never shouted, cheered or became enthusiastic, but steadily bore up his flag. At the battle of New Market cross roads, when every color-bearer in the division was either killed or wounded, Sergeant Blanchard received a wound in the arm, he retired a few minutes to have his wound bandaged and then returned to his place. At Antietam he was so severely wounded that the flag fell from his hands, and he was unable to raise it; Walter Beatty, a private, seized the banner to bear it aloft, and almost immediately fell dead, pierced by rebel bullets; another private, Robert Lemmon took the flag from the hands of his fallen comrade, a companion calling out to him, "don't touch it, Bob, or they'll kill you," the brave boy, however, bore up the banner, and in less than a minute lay dead on the ground; the colors were then taken by Edward Doran, a little Irishman, who lying upon his back, held up the flag till the end of the battle, and for his gallantry was made a non-commissioned officer on the field.'

Few things were more disgraceful than losing one's colours in battle, and extreme sacrifices were often made to save them. For example, the 1st Delaware Infantry Regiment were also at Antietam where they were stopped by overwhelming enemy fire, suffering heavy losses. They were driven back, caught between fire from enemy troops in their front and from reinforcements who confused them for Confederates in the fog of battle. Despite tremendous fire, according to the regiment's historian: 'On the ground, a few yards in advance, where the line was first arrested, lay a large number of our men, killed or wounded, and among them lay the colors of the regiment, one of which was held by Lieutenant-Colonel Hopkinson, who was wounded. Major Smyth, Captain Rickards, Lieutenants Postles, Tanner, and Nicholls, Sergeants Dunn and McAllister, with several other non-commissioned officers, rallied a large number of the men for the purpose of returning to the original line, recovering the colors, and holding the position, if possible.

'They sallied gallantly to the front under a terrible tornado of shot, and held the position for a considerable time. . . . When the regiment retired from the field both colors were brought with it, one by Lieutenant C.B. Tanner and the other by Sergeant Allen Tatem, one of the color-guard.'

Howard Michael Madaus, one of America's leading experts on Civil War flags, holds an authentically reconstructed national colour of the 2d Wisconsin Volunteer Infantry Regiment, which he carried at the 125th anniversary recreation of the battle of First Bull Run. He wears an authentically reconstructed 1861 Wisconsin uniform.

Select Bibliography

Beale, James, *The Battle Flags of the Army of the Potomac at Gettysburg, Penna, July 1st, 2d & 3d, 1863*, Philadelphia, 1885

Billings, John D., *Hardtack and Coffee*, Glendale, New York, 1970

Official, *Atlas to accompany the Official Records...*, Washington, DC, 1891–1895

Madaus, H. Michael, 'McClellan's System of Designating Flags, Spring-Fall, 1862'; *Military Collector & Historian*, Washington, DC, Spring 1965, pp 1–13

Madaus, Howard M., 'The Conservation of Civil War Flags: The Military Historian's Perspective'; *Papers presented at the Pennsylvania Capitol; Preservation Committee Flag Symposium, 1987*, Harrisburg, 1987

Phillips, Stanley S., *Civil War Corps Badges and Other Related Awards, Badges, Medals of the Period*, Lanham, Maryland, 1982

Sauers, Richard A., *Advance The Colors!*, Harrisburg, 1987

Todd, Frederick P., *American Military Equippage*, Vol II, Providence, Rhode Island, 1977

REGULATION FLAGS

The Army of the United States basically had two colours per dismounted regiment, which were issued according to army-wide regulations issued 10 August 1861. From the *Revised Regulations for the Army of the United States, 1861*:

'1436. The garrison flag is the national flag. It is made of bunting, thirty-six feet fly, the twenty feet hoist, in thirteen horizontal stripes of equal breadth, alternately red and white, beginning with the red. In the upper quarter, next to the staff, is the Union, composed of a number of white stars, equal to the number of States, on a blue field, one-third the length of the flag, extending to the lower edge of the fourth red stripe from the top. The storm flag is twenty feet by ten feet; the recruiting flag, nine feet nine inches by four feet four inches.

Colors of Artillery Regiments

'1437. Each regiment of Artillery shall have two silken colors. The first, or the national color, of stars and stripes, as described for the garrison flag. The number and name of the regiment to be embroidered with gold on the centre stripe. The second, or regimental color, to be yellow, of the same dimensions as the first, bearing in the center two cannon crossing, with the letters U.S. above, and the number of regiment below; fringe, yellow. Each color to be six feet inches fly, and six feet deep on the pike. The

The national colour behind this captain appears to be that of the Governor's Foot Guard, a uniformed but strictly social Connecticut organization. Nonetheless, it shows the eagle finial which often topped the national colour, and the tassels. (David Scheinmann Collection)

The national colour is carried in action in 1861. Note the eagle and streamers.

pike, including the spear and ferrule, to be nine feet ten inches in length. Cords and tassels, red and yellow silk intermixed.

Colors of Infantry Regiments

'1438. Each regiment of Infantry shall have two silken colors. The first, or the national color, of stars and stripes, as described for the garrison flag; the number and name of the regiment to be embroidered with silver on the center stripe. The second, or regimental color, to be blue, with the arms of the United States embroidered in silk on the center. The name of the regiment in a scroll, underneath the eagle. The size of each color to be six feet six inches fly, and six feet deep on the pike. The length of the pike, including the spear and ferrule, to be nine feet ten inches. The fringe yellow; cord and tassels, blue and white silk intermixed.

Camp Colors

'1439. The camp colors are of bunting, eighteen inches square; white for infantry, and red for artillery, with the number of the regiment on them. The pole eight feet long.'

Each foot regiment was to have two camp colours, carried on the extreme right and left of the regiment by sergeants serving as general guides. In fact many of the actual colours violated regulations by having unique insignia on them. The 72nd Pennsylvania Volunteer Infantry, for example, had plain dark blue camp colours with a golden bee painted on a sky blue oval; and the 95th Ohio Volunteer Infantry had scarlet silk camp colours with a golden wreath surrounding the unit designation, '95 OHIO'.

General Orders No. 4, 18 January 1862, said that 'camp colors ... will be made like the United States flag, with stars and stripes'. Surviving camp colours of the 128th New York Infantry were made in this style, with the number 128 on a dark blue cloth field, sewn onto the colour.

The star pattern in the canton of this national colour of the 18th US Infantry Regiment matches those made under a US Quartermaster

Department contract by Alexander Brandon, issued through the New York Quartermaster Depot in 1864. (West Point Museum Collections)

Manufacturers' variations

The description of the national flag used as a camp colour, as well as both a garrison and regimental flag in the regulations, was vague in such details as the exact arrangement of the stars in the canton. Indeed, it did not even spell out if the canton were to be square or rectangular. A variety of styles of canton shapes and star designs were seen in actual practice, varying according to the flags' makers.

One basic difference between Army national colours and flags flown by civilians and non-military governmental organizations is that most Army national colours used gold stars while most other American flags had white stars. Apparently this came about when the Army switched to silver embroidery for its stars before the war; silver embroidery thread tarnished to an unsightly black, so gold was substituted for silver—hence the gold stars. Many private manufacturers during the war did embroider white stars on the cantons of the national colours they supplied under state contracts, but Army-issued national colours had gold stars, usually painted rather than embroidered.

Army-issued national colours were provided to regiments which needed replacement colours or did not receive presentation colours from their state

government or local organizations. Army-issued colours were issued at the Quartermaster Depots in Philadelphia, New York, and Cincinnati, Ohio. Private contractors between May 1861 and October 1865 supplied the Philadelphia Depot with 890 national colours, the New York Depot with 917 national colours, and the Cincinnati Depot with 500 national colours.

National colours provided by the Philadelphia Depot apparently had the gold stars in their rectangular cantons arranged as a vertical double ellipse with an additional star in each corner. Some had a centre star, while some lacked this final star.

New York Depot national colours had the gold stars in a square canton arranged in five horizontal rows. Until 4 July 1863, when West Virginia was admitted as a new state and a new star was authorized for it, these had six stars in the middle row and seven stars in each of the two outer rows. After 4 July 1863 each row had seven stars. Although Nevada was admitted to the Union on 31 October 1864, no star was authorized to mark that state until after the war was over.

Apparently national colours supplied by the Cincinnati Depot had rectangular cantons with seven horizontal rows of gold stars. Each row except the bottom one had five stars, with four stars in the bottom row until July 1863, when it, too, acquired a fifth.

Most regiments, however, especially early in the war, were presented with national colours by some local group which had acquired them from private contractors. These colours were quite expensive by the standards of the day.

Pennsylvania's state inspector general asked for bids for making flags for the Commonwealth's troops from three local manufacturers. One, Horstmann, asked $160 for a pair of national and regimental colours, $35 for a cavalry standard, and $12 for a cavalry guidon. Evans & Hassall wanted $135 for a pair of national and regimental colours, $35 for a cavalry standard, and $22.50 for a cavalry guidon. Brewer wanted $110 for the infantry colours, $30 for the cavalry standard, and $15 for the guidon. (At this time a private soldier's pay was only $13 a month.)

On 27 November 1861 the adjutant general of Kentucky asked for quotes for making flags for the state's troops from both a local manufacturer, Hugh

Wilkins of Louisville, Kentucky, and Tiffany & Co. of New York City. Wilkins replied: 'I will make infantry regimental colors for $125 per set with the arms of Kentucky on each side of the standard and regular regimental flag stars and stripes with the number of each regiment in gold on each side and the same in the blue flag on a scroll under the coat of arms. Cavalry standards done in a like manner for $45.00 each, guidons for $10.00 each. Artillery flags same as Infantry.'

Tiffany wired: 'Blue regimentals both sides $100.00 each in three weeks, with case, belt, and fringe. National stars and stripes $60.00 each in one week. Guidons embroidered name and number $25.00 pair in two weeks.'

Presentation national colours made by Tiffany went mostly to New York and some Connecticut units, although some were carried by Michigan units and at least one by an Indiana unit. Tiffany colours were embroidered with white stars in a square canton. Until July 1863 they were set in six horizontal rows, the middle two with five stars while the outer two had six stars. Starting in July 1863 the top three rows had six stars each; the fourth row had five; and the bottom two rows had six. Unit designations on Tiffany colours were rendered in script letters.

Presentation national colours made by another New York maker, Paton & Company, used white silk appliquéd stars set in five horizontal rows, the middle one of which had six stars while the upper and lower two had seven stars each, in a square canton. The unit designation appeared in script letters.

Evans & Hassall of Philadelphia, Pennsylvania, arranged the gold stars in the rectangular cantons of their national colours as a simple double ellipse of stars surrounding a single star in the centre, with one gold star at each corner of the canton. New Jersey regiments after 1863 received national colours made by this company.

Horstmann Brothers & Co., a general military equipment and uniform supplier from Philadelphia, also produced presentation national colours for Minnesota troops for a short time starting in late 1862, and for West Virginia's troops after that state's formation. These were made like the Evans & Hassall colours with a double ellipse of gold stars in a rectangular canton. Both Evans & Hassall and Horstmann also produced national colours for Pennsylvania troops, but these differed in that the state seal surrounded by stars was painted in the centre of the canton. The first national colours supplied by Horstmann to New Jersey used this same design, with the New Jersey state seal surrounded by stars in their cantons.

Maryland troops received national colours made by Sisco Bros., of Baltimore, with square cantons and, after July 1863, five horizontal rows of seven gold stars each.

Hugh Wilkins, Louisville, Kentucky, produced national colours for Kentucky troops and, apparently, units from Illinois, Indiana, and Ohio as well. These were unusual in that a light or sky blue was used for the square cantons. The gold stars were arranged in six horizontal rows, five in the top and bottom rows and six in the other rows.

A private of the Veteran Reserve Corps, formed from men no longer capable of active field service but still capable of serving, holds one of the Corps' national colours. (Ronn Palm Collection)

Gilbert Hubbard & Co., Chicago, Illinois, made national colours for units from Wisconsin. Its first ones had the state seal as well as stars in the rectangular cantons. However, replacement colours made until July 1863 had gold stars in six horizontal rows with six in the top, bottom, and two middle rows and five in the second and fifth rows.

Regimental colours were also issued through the three basic quatermaster depots. Between May 1861 and October 1865 the Philadelphia Depot purchased 765 regimental colours; the New York Depot, 1,021 regimental colours; and the Cincinnati Depot, 564 regimental colours.

Many of Philadelphia's regimental colours came from Horstmann and Evans & Hassall. These colours bear the US coat of arms on the eagle's breast over a three-piece red scroll painted with a raised centre section and under a double curve of stars: the top row had 21 stars, the bottom row 13 stars.

New York's Depot had a variety of suppliers including A. Ertle, Paton & Co., and A. Brandon. They had a large, but somewhat unrealistic eagle under two rows of stars, 18 in the top row and 16 in the bottom.

Cincinnati's Depot had several contractors who provided regimental colours of various qualities.

An officer holds a battle-torn national colour bearing three battle honours for engagements in the Army of the Potomac. Note the axehead which tops the stave.

John Shilleto of Cincinnati turned out well-painted eagles with detailed feathers and realistic heads. His first colours had 21 stars in the top row over 13 stars in the bottom, ending at the tail of the motto scroll. His post-July 1863 colours had 20 stars over 15 stars in two rows which extended below the ends of the scroll.

Another Cincinnati supplier, Longly & Bro., turned out eagles which were poorly painted, with ill-defined feathers and a 'black eye' on each eagle's head. Until July 1863 the top row of stars on these flags had 21 stars, over 13 stars in the bottom row; after that date they bore 21 over 14 stars, the latter touching the trails of the motto scroll. The motto scrolls from both makers had lower centre sections.

Hugh Wilkins' regimental colours featured eagles with down-turned heads, as well as another design which had the eagle perched on a US shield in the centre of a circular clouded perch. Both had five-piece red motto scrolls.

Both national and regimental colours, save those presented by local groups and locally made, were issued without regimental designations in the stripe or motto scroll. It was up to each regimental colonel to have the regimental designation put on each colour.

* * *

To return to the 1861 Army Regulations:
'Standards and Guidons of Mounted Regiments
'1440. Each regiment will have a silken standard, and each company a silken guidon. The standard to bear the arms of the United States, embroidered in silk, on a blue ground, with the number and name of the regiment, in a scroll underneath the eagle. The flag of the standard to be two feet five inches wide, and two feet three inches on the lance, and to be edged with yellow silk fringe.
'1441. The flag of the guidon is swallow-tailed, three feet five inches from the lance to the end of the swallow-tail; fifteen inches to the fork of the swallow-tail, and two feet three inches on the lance. To be half red and half white, dividing at the fork, the red above.

On the red, the letters U.S. in white; and on the white, the letter of the company in red. The lance of the standards and guidons to be nine feet long, including spear and ferrule.'

Modifications to the 1861 regulations appeared soon after they were published. The first changed the guidons issued to mounted units. According to General Orders No. 4, issued 18 January 1862: '1. Under instructions from the Secretary of War, dated January 7, 1862, guidons and camp colors for the Army will be made like the United States flag, with stars and stripes.'

Mounted units wanted to fly a version of the US national flag. However, not even the modification of January 1862, which gave them a guidon version of the US flag, was enough for many such units; instead, they often flew the whole US flag. Indeed, a message from the commander of the Army of the Ohio, dated 3 June 1862, to Brigadier General Thomas Critten-den noted: 'The general yesterday observed one of the batteries in your division carrying a large flag

A colour-sergeant holding his battle-torn flag. The regiment is unknown. (Ronn Palm Collection)

61

This national colour used in Virginia in 1861 displays a different star pattern from that usually employed. There were no clear national regulations on the arrangement of stars.

the regular army. But the volunteers seemed to be a law unto themselves, and, while many flags in existence today bear names of battles inscribed by order of the commanding general, there are some with inscriptions of battles which the troops were hardly in hearing of.'

Table A: Unit Designations

Unit designations on national colours were placed on one of the horizontal stripes, often the seventh one from the top. However, this system was far from universal, as seen by the selection of representative national colours which have survived and are listed below. When the stripe is indicated it is counted from the top down. When letters or an abbreviation follow the number or capital letters, such as '2d' or 'REGt', the small letter was usually raised parallel with the top of the larger numbers and one or two dots placed under the small letter.

Unit designation	Designation placement
1st BATn PIONEER BRIGADE	7th stripe
2nd MICH. INF.	7th stripe
2d Wisconsin Infantry Volunteers.	7th stripe
3rd REGt WIS. VETERAN INFANTRY.	7th stripe
7th REGt NEW JERSEY VOLUNTEERS.	7th stripe
13th ILL.	7th stripe
15th REGt Ky VOLs	8th stripe
15th REGt WIS. VOLs.	7th stripe
15th REGt IND. VOLS.	9th stripe
18th Michigan Infantry.	7th stripe
19th REGIMENT/ MASSACHUSETTS VOLs	5th/7th stripes
MASSACHUSETTS VOLUNTEERS/21st. REGT. INFANTRY	4th/6th stripes
28th REG. PENNa VOL. INFy	7th stripe
40th REGt N.J. VOLS.	7th stripe
46th Regt. MASS. MILITIA	7th stripe
46th REGT. O.V.I.	3rd stripe
46th Ohio V.V.I.	Centre of canton
51st REG'T P.V.V.	Top stripe
56th Regiment,/ MASSACHUSETTS VOLs.	5th/7th stripes
60th REG'T O.V.U.S.A.	7th stripe
68th REGT. OHIO VET. VOL. INFANTRY	8th stripe
76th OHIO	7th stripe
154th Regt. NYSV (in script)	7th stripe

instead of a guidon, as ordered. The general desires to know why the orders on this subject are not carried out.'

Battle honours

Shortly after the guidon revision order was issued a practice that had been standard for many years before the war was made official. Regiments and batteries were allowed to indicate their service in battle on their colours. As stated in General Orders No. 19, 22 February 1862: 'It has been ordered that there shall be inscribed upon the colors or guidons of all regiments and batteries in the service of the United States the names of the battle in which they have borne a meritorious part.' The order went on to say that 'It is expected that troops so distinguished will regard their colors as representing the honor of their corps—to be lost only with their lives—and that those not yet entitled to such a distinction will not rest satisfied until they have won it by their discipline and courage.'

This privilege was soon abused by a number of volunteer units which put the names of battles in which they had played the most minor of parts onto their colours. According to John Billings, a veteran of the 10th Massachusetts Artillery, in the Army of the Potomac, 'Originally battles were only inscribed on flags by authority of the secretary of war, that is, in

This was not always the fault of the troops who carried the colours; it was often unclear what unit was authorized what battle honour. Some commanders published lists of battle honours that could be placed on flags, some simply ordered every unit present at any given battle to put the honour on its flag. Even some governors issued orders to their state units to put specific honours on their battle flags.

As a result of this confusion, on 7 March 1865 the Army of the Potomac issued its General Orders No. 10 which listed every volunteer unit in the army along with a list of battles that could be placed on its colours. However, the Army of the Potomac appears to have been the only large organization within the Union forces to attempt to standardize battle honours and, by the time it did so, many of its older units had already been mustered out, their battle flags now hanging in state capital buildings.

* * *

Finally, according to the 1861 regulations: 'The ambulance depot, to which the wounded are carried or directed for immediate treatment, is generally established at the most convenient building nearest the field of battle. A *red flag* marks its place, or the way to it, to the conductors of the ambulances and to

the wounded who can walk.' General hospital flags were in fact yellow, with a large green Roman letter H on the field, and smaller yellow flags with green borders were generally used to mark the way from the firing line to field hospitals. This was standardized by General Orders No. 9, 4 January 1864, which called for a yellow general hospital flag 5 ft. by 9 ft. in size with a Roman letter H, 24 inches tall, on its field. Post and field hospitals had the same flag although only 5 ft. by 9 ft. in size. Rectangular guidons 14 inches by 28 inches edged with one-inch green borders were to mark ambulances as well as the route to field hospitals.

ARMY HEADQUARTERS FLAGS

No special colours were authorized under the regulations for army headquarters. Yet there was a precedent for having a special flag for marking the headquarters of a commanding general; during the War for American Independence, George Washington's headquarters was marked by an all-blue flag bearing 13 five-pointed stars.

In fact, the first flag selected to mark the headquarters of the Army of the Potomac, under General Orders No. 102, 24 March 1862, was a plain national flag. The national flag used by the army's headquarters in 1863, now in the Military Order of the Loyal Legion of the US, Philadelphia, had four rows of seven stars over a last row of six stars in its canton. It was 4 ft. on the hoist by 5½ ft. in the fly. It bears no unit designation or other distinctive marks.

Indeed, veteran John Billings later recalled that 'The stars and stripes were a common flag for army headquarters. It was General Meade's headquarters till Grant came to the Army of the Potomac, who also used it for that purpose.' Therefore, on 2 May 1864

A colour-sergeant of the 141st Pennsylvania Volunteer Infantry Regiment sits in front of the regiment's national and regimental colours. The regimental colour tassel hangs over his right shoulder. (Ronn Palm Collection)

This infantry regimental colour conforms in overall design to those known to have been issued by the New York Quartermaster Depot. The regiment that received it would have been responsible for getting the number filled in properly. (West Point Museum Collections)

the army's final commander, Major-General George G. Meade, adopted a new headquarters flag. According to an army circular issued at that time, 'Hereafter the designating flag for these headquarters will be a magenta-colored swallow tailed flag, with an eagle in gold, surrounded by a silver wreath for an emblem.' Billings said the guidon was actually 'lilac colored'. It measured 4 ft. on the hoist by 6 ft. on the fly (see *MAA 179*, p. 25).

The Army of the Potomac's Artillery Reserve had its own flag, authorized in General Orders No. 119, 30 April 1862. This was a 5 ft. by 6 ft. rectangular red flag with a white star in its centre. This was changed by General Orders No. 53, 12 May 1863, to a red swallow-tailed guidon, of the same dimensions as other corps flags, with a pair of white crossed cannon on its centre. Brigadier-General Henry J. Hunt, Army of the Potomac chief of artillery, apparently adopted a blue guidon with a red Roman letter A surmounting a pair of white crossed cannon for a personal flag in 1864. In October 1864 the Horse Artillery Brigade received a blue triangular flag with red crossed cannon, and the letters H above the cannon and A under them.

Other Army of the Potomac generals flew their own flags. The flag of the chief of engineers, for example, was a blue field, 4 ft. by 6 ft., with a red turreted castle, the symbol of the Corps of Engineers (see *MAA 179*, p. 28).

The Army of the James was created from the X and XVIII Corps in 1864. On 3 May 1864 its headquarters adopted a 6 ft.-square flag divided horizontally into red and blue halves. A large five-pointed star in white was placed in the centre.

When Major-General Philip Sheridan received command of the Army of the Shenandoah he appears to have used a swallow-tailed cavalry guidon to mark his headquarters. The guidon was divided into horizontal halves, the top white and the bottom red. A red five-pointed star was placed on the top half, and a similar star in white on the bottom half. The guidon measured some 3 ft. on the hoist by 6 ft. on the fly.

Under General Orders No. 91, Department of the Cumberland, the flag for department and army headquarters was a national flag 'with a golden eagle below the stars, two feet from tip to tip'. The flag's size was 5 ft. by 6 ft. However, according to General Orders No. 62, 26 April 1864, the headquarters flag was to be a 5 ft.-square national colour; it bore the gold Roman letters 'D.C.' within the canton and a gold eagle clutching a laurel branch in its left claw and five arrows in its right. The motto 'E PLURIBUS UNUM' flew from its beak. The eagle was painted on the field no deeper than the canton. The placement of the eagle is slightly different on the reverse from the obverse.

The Department and the Army of Tennessee and the Army of the Ohio had very similar headquarters flags, both with blue fields and gold fringe, cords and tassels. The Army of Tennessee's flag had the corps badges of the XV and XVII Corps on a vertical background of red, white, and blue. The flag of the Army of the Ohio had the corps badges of the X and XXIII Corps, suspended from sabres, topped by an eagle which looked very much like the colonel's rank badge. It would appear that these two headquarters flags were adopted after they joined the forces under Major-General William T. Sherman in North Carolina in the dying days of the war.

The Military Division of the Mississippi apparently used a 5 ft.-square plain yellow flag as its headquarters flag. In early 1865 the badges adopted by the corps within the division were painted on it.

THE ARMY OF THE POTOMAC

As the Union's field armies grew in size, various of their commanders attempted to make units easy to identify in the field through systems of unique flags carried by each formation and unit. The Army of the Potomac's General Orders No. 102 was issued 24 March 1862, under Major-General George B. McClellan's direction, and gave the Union Army its first comprehensive army-wide flag designating system.

According to the sections which provided instructions on flags, the army's general headquarters would be marked by a plain national flag. Corps headquarters would have a national flag with a small square flag, of a different colour or set of colours, on the same staff under the national flag. The I Corps flag was to be red; II Corps, blue; III Corps, blue and red in vertical halves; and IV Corps, blue and red in horizontal halves.

All divisions had the same size flags, 6 ft. long and 5 ft. wide. The first division of an army corps had a red flag; the second division blue; the third division a vertically divided red and blue flag (contemporary illustrations show that the red half was on the hoist side and the blue on the fly); and the fourth division a horizontally divided red and blue flag.

In fact, however, period writers do not mention any fourth divisions or their flags in the Army of the Potomac for the period. Colonel Charles Wainwright jotted this description in his diary only two days after the new order setting up the flag system was issued: 'One of the first (orders) prescribes the powers of corps commanders, and also designates flags for each headquarters. First Division's [*sic*] will carry a red flag 6 by 5; Second Division's blue; Third Division's red and blue vertical. Ours being the Second will have a blue flag.'

The brigades within each division were marked by different flags, each the same size as the division headquarters flag. Within each first division, the first brigade had a red and white flag in vertical stripes; the second, vertical white, red, and white stripes; and the third, vertical red, white, and red stripes.

The colour guard of the 36th Massachusetts Volunteer Infantry Regiment hold their well-worn colours in this picture dating from late in the war. The two general guides hold their camp colours on either end of the line; these would have flown at either flank of the regiment to mark its position. (US Army Military History Institute)

Within each corps' second division, the first brigade had a vertical striped blue and white flag; the second brigade had vertical white, blue, and white stripes; the third, vertical blue, white, and blue stripes.

The same sized flags were used by brigade headquarters in each corps' third division. The first brigade had vertical red, white, and blue stripes; the second, vertical red, blue, and white stripes; and the third, vertical white, red, and blue stripes.

Among corps with a fourth division, the first brigade had horizontal red, white, and blue stripes; the second, horizontal red, blue, and white stripes; and the third, horizontal white, red, and blue stripes.

Within each brigade, each regiment was to carry in addition to its national and regimental colours a copy of the brigade headquarters flag with the numbers 1, 2, 3 or 4 on it, according to the unit's ranking on the brigade table of organization. White numbers were used on coloured bars and coloured numbers (which often appear to have been red) on white bars. Actual regimental flags measure between

54 and 56 inches on the hoist and between 70 and 72 inches on the fly.

Artillery batteries were to carry the colours of the division to which they belonged as well as a right-angled triangular flag 6 ft. long and 3 ft. wide at the staff. Cavalry units were to have the same as the artillery, although their flag was to be swallow-tailed. Engineer units had a white disc of a diameter equal to one third of its width on the flag of the division to which the unit was assigned.

The Regular Brigade had a white star on a red flag, the regimental number being in the middle of the star. This was changed by General Order No. 119, 30 April 1862, to a 'blue flag with a white star in the center'. In fact, an original flag carried in the brigade is at the Chapel of St. Cornelius the Centurion, Ft. Jay, New York. It is only 18 inches long on the hoist and 3 ft. on the fly, with a white star within an oval green laurel wreath. This flag, carried during the Peninsular Campaign, became the head-quarters flag of the 2d Division, Provisional V Corps, in May 1862 when the brigade was made part of that corps.

Hospitals were distinguished by a yellow flag. As described above, hospital flags were also marked with a Roman letter H in green, and small rectangular guidons of yellow edged with green were used to

A pair of regimental colours in action, 27 June 1862, during the Peninsular Campaign. The national colour is topped with an eagle while the regimental colour has a spike finial. They are both carried in the front and centre of the regimental front.

The regimental colour of the 1st Veteran Reserve Corps Regiment conforms in design to those made by Longly & Bros. under Quartermaster Department contract through the Cincinnati Depot. The 18th Veteran Reserve Corps Regiment regimental colour, however, was made by Horstmann Bros. for the Philadelphia Depot and differs slightly in design. (West Point Museum Collections)

mark the way from the front line to the field hospitals. Subsistence depots were designated by a green flag.

These flags were attached to a portable staff 14 feet long, in two joints, and were supposed to be habitually displayed in front of the headquarters which they designated. On the march they were to be carried near the unit commander.

These orders were modified by General Orders No. 110, 26 March 1862:

'Third Army Corps: National flag with a small square red and blue (instead of blue and red) flag, vertical, beneath.

'Fourth Army Corps: National flag with a small square red and blue (instead of blue and red) flag, horizontal, beneath.'

They were further modified in General Orders No. 119, 30 April 1862, which gave the cavalry reserve headquarters a yellow flag 6 ft. long and 5 ft. wide, with two blue stripes 6 inches in width, crossing

The regimental colour bearers for the 111th Pennsylvania Volunteer Infantry Regiment. At the end of the war it was quite popular for units to have their colours photographed so that members could keep the images as mementoes of their service. Note the spearpoint finial on the regimental colour. (Ronn Palm Collection)

diagonally. The reserve's first brigade had a yellow flag the same size, with one blue star in the centre, while the second brigade had the same flag with two blue stars in the centre. The artillery reserve headquarters received a similar sized red flag with a white star in the centre, while the brigade of regular infantry received a blue flag of the same size with a white star in the centre.

An additional flag was made regulation by General Orders No. 152, 9 August 1862: 'The main (ordnance) depot for the army will be designated by a crimson flag, marked "Ordnance Depot, U.S.A."'

Although the system was all-inclusive, there is some question as to what degree it was actually practised. Regiments tended to get transferred between brigades quite often, meaning that they had to change flags just as often. Moreover, there was bound to be less loyalty to such an arbitrary and abstract flag than to the elaborate regimental and national colours which were distinguished with the unit's actual designation. Even so, there are a number of surviving examples of regimental designating flags, so many must have seen actual use.

On 25 November 1862, after the V Corps was added to the Army of the Potomac, Brigadier-General Daniel Butterfield of that corps wrote to army headquarters: 'In the order designating flags for

A pre-1863 regimental colour for the 5th US Artillery Regiment, with the design smaller in the field than after 1863. (West Point Museum Collections)

a system of badges unique to each division of each corps, worn on the soldier's hat or coat breast. These unique badges were adapted to a revised system of identification flags carried by divisions and brigades which was made official by General Orders No. 53, dated 12 May 1863.

The cavalry corps headquarters was now to carry a flag of the same size and shape as had been used by infantry corps, but all in yellow with white crossed sabres on its centre. The artillery reserve headquarters flag was to be the same, but in red with white crossed cannon in its centre.

Each division headquarters was to fly a different style flag. Each corps' first division was to have a white rectangular flag with a red corps badge in its centre; the second division had a blue flag with a white corps badge; the third, a white flag with a blue corps badge.

The VI Corps' 'light division' had a white rectangular flag, with a green Greek cross in its centre.

The brigades in each corps' first division had a white triangular flag with a red corps badge in the centre. The first brigade simply carried this colour; the second brigade had an additional 6-inch-wide blue stripe next to the staff; the third, a $4\frac{1}{2}$-inch blue border all around the flag. According to Billings, 'Whenever there was a fourth brigade, it was designated by a triangular block of color in each corner of the flag.'

The brigades of each corps' second division had a blue triangular flag with a white corps badge in the centre. The individual brigade flags used the same system as in the first division, the stripes and borders being red instead of blue.

The brigades of each corps' third division had a white triangular flag with a blue corps badge in the centre. Individual brigade flags used the same system as the first division, the stripe and borders being red.

Although not mentioned in the initial order, soon after it was issued corps artillery headquarters adopted a red brigade flag with the corps badge in white in its centre. The corps quartermaster's headquarters had a blue swallow-tailed guidon the same size as the brigade flags with diagonal white stripes parallel with the swallow tails and ending at the top and bottom of the flag at the staff.

This system of flags to designate specific head-

Army Corps (orders 102 and 110, Headquarters, Army of the Potomac, March 1862) no flag has been designated for the Fifth Corps.

'I would respectfully request that a flag be designated as shown in the following sketch. For the Fifth Army Corps, viz: Red with a Greek Cross in the center, under the national flag as per General Orders No. 102, Army of the Potomac, and that the Quartermaster's Department be directed to furnish the same.'

Butterfield's sketch did not in fact show a Greek cross, but a cross *botonée*, which is a form of Greek cross save that each arm ends in a trefoil bud.

On 7 February 1863, according to General Orders No. 10, the corps headquarters flags were changed to blue swallow-tailed guidons 6 ft. on the fly by 2 ft. on the hoist, each with a white cross bearing the corps number in red Roman numerals in the centre of the cross. According to the order, the cross was to be a 'Maltese cross', but actual examples show it to have been the cross *botonée* that Butterfield, who designed the corps badges later used in the Army of the Potomac, earlier suggested for the V Corps.

When Major-General Joseph Hooker took over the demoralized Army of the Potomac after the defeat at Fredericksburg and its 'mud march', he began to restore the army's morale. In part he did this through

quarters in the Army of the Potomac continued in use through the army's existence.

Corps Badges of the Army of the Potomac, 1863

Corps	Badge
I	A sphere
II	A trefoil
III	A lozenge
V	A Maltese cross
VI	A (Greek) cross
IX*	A shield with a figure 9 in the centre, crossed with a fouled anchor and cannon
X*	A four-bastioned fort
XXI*	A crescent, points up
XII*	A five-pointed star

(*Served with the Army of the Potomac at one time or another but was not always a member of that army.)

The IX Corps adopted a fairly complicated badge which did not lend itself to the simple outline style of badge used by the other corps. It involved a cannon crossing a fouled anchor on a shield. Therefore, when the IX Corps adopted its flags to conform with the Army of the Potomac system on 1 August 1864, it called for flags that were slightly more elaborate than those used by the other corps. The headquarters' blue swallow-tailed guidon had a white shield with a red cannon crossing a blue anchor. The first division's blue shield had a blue cannon crossing a white anchor; the second division's white shield had a red cannon crossing a blue anchor; and the third division's blue shield had a white cannon crossing a red anchor.

Towards the end of the war, casualties forced units to be merged, even at corps level. On 26 November 1864 the merger of troops of the remainder of I Corps into Third Division, V Corps resulted in General Orders No. 10 which read in part, 'The Division flag will be the flag now authorized, with a circular belt surrounding the corps, insignia and of the same color.'

On 25 March 1864 the First Division, III Corps became the Third Division, II Corps, and the Second Division, III Corps became the Fourth Division, II Corps. However, Major-General A. A. Humphries, last commander of II Corps, later wrote, 'No power on earth could consolidate or fuse the Third with the Second, and the authorities were at length compelled to let the Old Third wear their Old Third insignia. The men would not discard the Lozenge or Diamond, and Mott's division headquarters flag, The Old Third, bore a white Trefoil on a blue Diamond or Lozenge on its swallow-tail.'

A post-war Quartermaster Department illustration of the regulation artillery regimental colour.

The regimental colour of the 1st US Artillery Regiment fits the style of colours made in 1863 and afterwards. (West Point Museum Collections)

The standard of the 2d US Cavalry Regiment. (West Point Museum Collections)

The Army of the James

The Army of the James was created on 2 April 1864 under Major-General Benjamin F. Butler with the purpose of attacking Richmond from the South. It was created with the X and XVIII Corps, which were discontinued on 3 December 1864 when the XXIV and XXV Corps replaced them.

On 3 May 1864 Army headquarters set up a fairly simple system of flag identification through division level. Headquarters used a 6 ft.-square flag divided horizontally red over blue; a large white five-pointed star was placed centrally on the field. The two colours in the field represented the two corps under its command.

According to an order sent to the X Corps commander on 3 May 1864 from the headquarters of the Department of Virginia and North Carolina: 'By direction of the commanding general of the department, I have the honor to submit the following explanation of the battle-flags to be used by the troops of this command during the coming campaign: The flag carried by department headquarters will be 6 feet square, two horizontal bars, upper bar red, lower bar blue, with a white star in the center; the flag carried by the headquarters Eighteenth Army Corps will be 6 feet square, blood red, with number "18" in the center; First Division flag, same size, blood red, with a single white star in the center; Second Division

flag, same size and color, with two white stars in the center; Third Division flag, same size and color, with three white stars in the center. The flag carried by the Tenth Army Corps will be 6 feet square, dark blue, with the number "10" in the center; First Division flag, same size and color, with a single white star in the center; Second Division flag, same size and color, with two white stars in the center; Third Division, same size and color, with three white stars in the center. Brigade colors will be furnished as soon as practicable.'

This system was abandoned when the XXIV and XXV Corps replaced the original corps in the Army. Both of these corps used Army of the Potomac-style headquarters flags: dark blue swallow-tailed guidons, with a white corps badge and the corps number in red Roman numerals. The XXIV Corps badge was a heart, while that of the XXV Corps was a square. Their division flags were the same as in the Army of the Potomac at that time: white for the first and third divisions, and dark blue for the second division. The corps badge was placed on the field of each, red in the first division, white in the second division, and blue in the third division. Flag sizes in the two corps, however, varied. Division flags in the XXIV Corps were 4 ft. 6 ins. on the hoist by 6 ft. In the XXV Corps they were only 2 ft. 7 ins. by 5 ft. 9 in.

The Department of the Cumberland

On 19 December 1962 General Orders No. 41 was issued by the headquarters XIV Corps and the Department of the Cumberland in Nashville, Tennessee, which divided the forces in the department into 'the center' or 'wings'. Brigades and divisions were assigned into these groups to be numbered from right to left, although referred to by commanders' names in operational reports.

The same order indicated a system of flags to identify the headquarters of these commands:

'III. Flags will be used to indicate the various headquarters, as follows: General headquarters—the National flag, 6 feet by 5, with a golden eagle below the stars, 2 feet from tip to tip. Right wing—a plain light crimson flag. Center—a plain light blue flag. Left wing—a plain pink flag. First Division, right wing—the flag of the wing, with one white star, 18 inches in diameter, the inner point 1 inch from the staff. Second Division, right wing—the flag of the wing, with two white stars, each 18 inches in diameter, the inner points 1 inch from the staff. Third Division, right wing—the flag of the wing, with three white stars, each 18 inches in diameter, set in triangular form, the outside star 1 inch from the outer line of flag. The division flags of the center and left wing will correspond with the above; that is to say, they will be the flags of the center or left wing, as the case may be, and with one, two, or three white stars, each 18 inches in diameter, according as they represent the First, Second, or Third Divisions. The headquarters flags of all brigades will be the flags of their divisions, with the number of the brigade in black, 8 inches long, in the center of each star. That of the brigade of regulars, however, will, instead of the white star and black number, have simply a golden star. The flags of the wings will be 6 feet on staff by 4 feet fly; those of divisions and brigades 5 feet by 3.

They will all be of a pattern to be furnished to the quartermaster's department. Artillery reserve—a plain red flag, equilateral in shape, each side being 5 feet. Cavalry reserve—of the same shape as division flags, 3 feet fly by 5 on the staff, but of deep orange color. Divisions and brigades to be designated as in the infantry; that is, the First, Second, and Third Divisions by one, two, and three white stars respec-

Charging cavalrymen in 1864 carry regulation guidons.

A regulation cavalry guidon carried by an L Troop. (West Point Museum Collections)

tively; the First, Second, and Third Brigades by black figures in each star. Engineer Corps—a white and blue flag, blue uppermost and running horizontally. Flag 5 feet on staff by 3 feet fly. Hospitals and ambulance depots—a light yellow flag, 3 feet square, for the hospitals and for the principal ambulance depot on a field of battle; 2 feet square for the lesser ones. Subsistence depots or store-houses—a plain light green flag, 3 feet square. Quartermaster's depots or store houses—same flag, with the letters Q.M.D. in white, 1 foot long.

'IV. All of these flags will be attached to a portable staff, 14 feet long, made in two joints, and will be habitually displayed in front of the tent, or from some prominent part of the house or vessel occupied by the officer, whose headquarters they are intended to designate; and on the march will be carried near his person.'

This system apparently failed, for General Orders No. 91, issued by the Department of the Cumberland headquarters on 25 April 1863, stated:

'It having been found that the flags prescribed by General Orders, No. 41, from this headquarters, December 19, 1862, to designate the headquarters of the various brigades, divisions, and corps of this army, are not sufficiently marked to be readily distinguished from each other, those herein described will be substituted.

General headquarters The national flag, 6 feet by 5, with a golden eagle below the stars, 2 feet from tip to tip.

Fourteenth Army Corps A bright blue flag, 6 feet by 4, fringed, with black eagle in center, 2 feet from tip to tip, with the number "14" in black on shield, which shall be white.

Twentieth Army Corps A bright red flag, same as that for Fourteenth Army Corps, except the number on the shield, which shall be that of the corps.

Twenty-first Army Corps A bright red, white, and blue flag (horizontal), same as that for Fourteenth Corps, except the number on the shield, which shall be that of the corps.

First Division, Fourteenth Army Corps The flag of the corps, except the eagle and fringe, with one black star, 18 inches in diameter, point 2 inches from staff.

Second Division, Fourteenth Army Corps The flag of the corps, except eagle and fringe, with two black stars, each 18 inches in diameter, inner point 2 inches from staff.

Third Division, Fourteenth Army Corps The flag of the corps, except eagle and fringe, with three black stars, each 18 inches in diameter, set equally along staff, the inner point being 2 inches from staff.

Fourth Division, Fourteenth Army Corps The flag of the corps, except eagle and fringe, with four black stars, each 18 inches in diameter, three of them along

This regulation cavalry guidon was carried by the Cleveland Guards, officially known as L Troop, 1st Rhode Island Cavalry Regiment. (North Carolina Museum of History)

The 1864 headquarters flag of the Department of the Cumberland measures 4 by 4½ ft. The painted eagle is gold, as are the letters 'D.C.' (West Point Museum Collections)

staff as before, the other set equally on the flag.

Fifth Division, Fourteenth Army Corps The flag of the corps, except eagle and fringe, with five black stars, each 18 inches in diameter, three of them along the staff, the other two equally distributed on flag.

The division flags of the Twentieth and Twenty-first Army Corps will correspond with the above, that is, the corps flags (without eagle and fringe), with one, two, three, &c., stars, according as they represent the first, second, third, &c., divisions.

The headquarters flags of all brigades will be the flags of their divisions, with the number of the brigade in white, 8 inches long, in center of each star.

The Regular brigade will have the corps and division flag, but the stars shall be golden instead of black.

Artillery reserve Two bright red flags, each 4 feet by 2, one above the other.

Batteries Each battery shall have a small flag, corps colors, and arrangement (but 1 foot 6 inches on staff, by 2 feet fly), with the letters and numbers of the battery inscribed thereon in black, 4 inches long, thus, "B, First Ohio."

Cavalry headquarters A bright red, white, and blue flag, 6 feet by 4, colors running vertically, red outermost.

First Cavalry Division A bright red, white, and blue flag, 6 feet by 4, like last, with one star, 18 inches in diameter, black, the point 2 inches from staff.

Second Cavalry Division Same as last, except two black stars, each 18 inches in diameter.

'As for infantry, the headquarters flags of brigades will be the flags of divisions, with the number of the brigade in black, 8 inches long.

Engineer Corps A white and blue flag, blue uppermost, and running horizontally, 6 feet by 4.

Hospitals and ambulance depots A light yellow flag, 3 feet by 3, for hospitals and the principal ambulance depot on the field of battle, 2 feet square for the lesser ones.

Subsistence depots and storehouses A plain light green flag, 3 feet square.

Quartermaster's depots or storehouses Same flag, with letters Q.M.D. in white, 1 foot long.

Ordnance department, general headquarters A bright

green flag, 3 feet square, with two crossed cannon in white, set diagonally in a square of 3 feet, with a circular ribbon of 6 inches wide and 3 feet greatest diameter (or diameter of inner circle 2 feet), with the letters "U.S. Ordnance Department," in black, 4 inches long, on ribbon, and a streamer above flag, 1 foot on staff by 4 feet long, crimson color, with words "Chief of Ordnance" in black, 6 inches long.

Division ordnance Same flag, with cannon and ribbon, but no streamer.'

The XIX Corps

The XIX Corps included all the troops stationed in the Department of the Gulf between 5 January 1863 and 20 March 1865. On 18 February 1863 Department headquarters issued General Orders No. 17 which designated unique flags within the Corps:

'III. The various headquarters of the Department of the Gulf will be designated by small flags or guidons, 4 feet square, attached to a lance 12 feet long, made in two joints, as follows:

William McIlvaine, a soldier in the Army of the Potomac, sketched the headquarters of General Andrew Humphreys, 3d Division, V Corps, near Falmouth, Virginia on 30 March 1863. The identifying flag made regulation by General McClellan is on the smaller flagpole. It is halved red and blue, the red towards the hoist and the blue towards the fly. (National Archives)

1: National Colour, 3d US Inf. Regt.

2: National Colour, 1st Bn., 11th US Inf. Regt.
3: Regimental Colour, 6th US Inf. Regt.

1

2

3

A

1: Regimental Colour: 164th NY Inf. Regt.
2: Standard, 2d US Cav. Regt.
3: Regimental Colour, 5th US Arty. Regt.
4: Regimental Colour, artillery

1

2

3

4

B

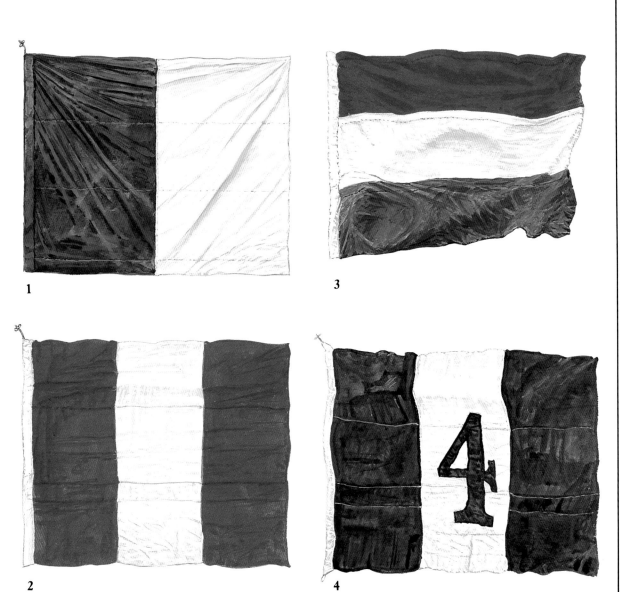

Designating flags, Army of the Potomac
1: 1st Bde., 2d Div. of a Corps
2: 3d Bde., 1st Div. of a Corps
3: 1st Bde., 4th Div. of a Corps
4: 11th Penn. Volunteer Inf. Regt.

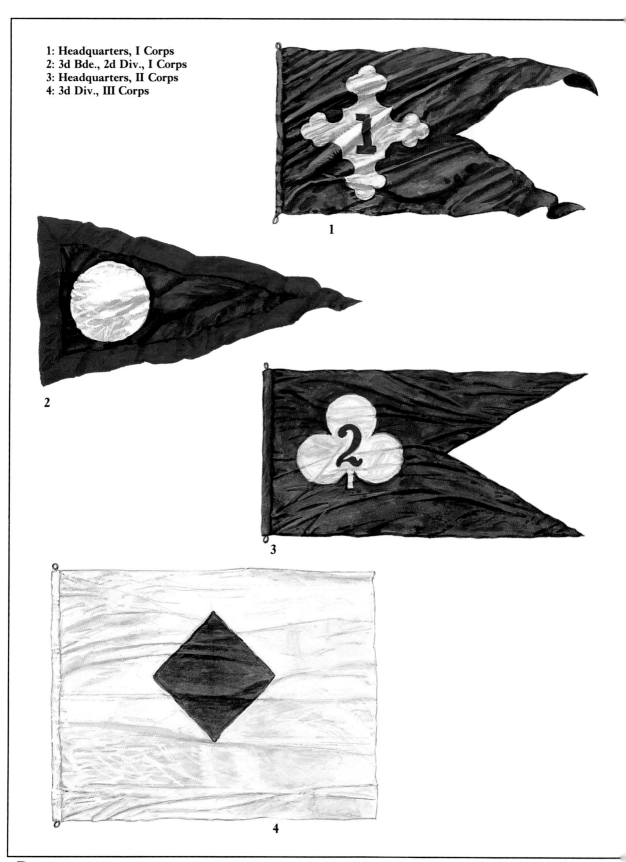

1: Headquarters, I Corps
2: 3d Bde., 2d Div., I Corps
3: Headquarters, II Corps
4: 3d Div., III Corps

D

1: 2d Div., V Corps
2: 1st Div., VI Corps
3: Headquarters, IX Corps
4: Headquarters, X Corps

E

1: Headquarters, XXIV Corps
2: Headquarters, XXIII Corps
3: Headquarters, XV Corps
4: 2d Div., XVIII Corps

1

3

2

4

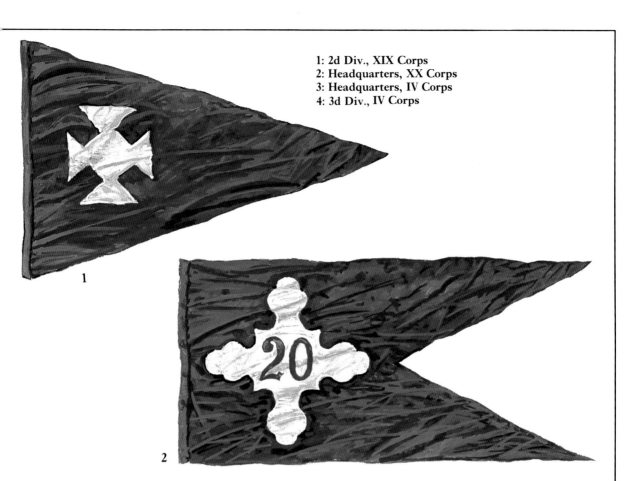

1: 2d Div., XIX Corps
2: Headquarters, XX Corps
3: Headquarters, IV Corps
4: 3d Div., IV Corps

1

2

3

4

1: Co., I, 6th Penn. Cavalry
2: Headquarters, XXI Corps
3: Headquarters, Cavalry Corps, Army of the Potomac

H

This elaborate flag marks the headquarters of the 2d Brigade, 4th Division, IX Corps, and dates from 1864. Its stripes are, from hoist, green, blue, and red, with a red number '2' and a white shield. The anchor is blue and the cannon red. It measures $2\frac{1}{2}$ by 4 ft. (West Point Museum Collections)

'The headquarters of the Nineteenth Army Corps and the Department of the Gulf by a flag, with a white four-pointed star in the center; the figure 19, in red, in the star.

'Division headquarters, red, with a white four-pointed star in the center; the number of the division in black figures in the star.

'Brigade headquarters, blue, white and horizontal stripes of equal width, the number of the brigade in black figures in the white stripes.'

General Orders No. 11, dated 17 November 1864, indicated both the corps badge and a unique set of flags for the XIX Corps:

'The flags will be as follows: For the headquarters of the corps, blue swallow-tail, seventy-two inches in length by thirty-nine on staff, with white cross eighteen inches square. For the headquarters of divisions, triangular, sixty-six inches in length by forty-four in staff, with cross fifteen inches square. First Division, red, with white cross; Second Division, blue, with white cross; Third Division, white, with blue cross. For the headquarters of brigade, rectangular, thirty-six inches in length by thirty on staff with cross fifteen inches square. First Brigade, First Division, blue and white, horizontal (blue underneath), red cross; Second Brigade, First Division, blue and red, horizontal (blue underneath), with cross; Third Brigade, First Division, red and white, horizontal (red underneath), blue cross; First

Brigade, Second Division, blue and white, perpendicular (blue on staff), red cross; Second Brigade, Second Division, blue and red, perpendicular (blue on staff), white cross; Third Brigade, Second Division, red and white, perpendicular (red on staff), blue cross; Fourth Brigade, Second Division, blue and red, perpendicular (red on staff), white cross; First Brigade, Third Division, blue and white, diagonal (blue on staff), red cross; Second Brigade, Third Division, blue and red, diagonal (blue on staff), white cross; Third Brigade, Third Division, red and white, diagonal (red on staff), blue cross.'

The XXIII Corps

The XXIII Corps, created 27 April 1863 from troops in Kentucky in the Department of Ohio, also served in the Department of North Carolina until disbanded 1 August 1865. Special Field Orders No. 121, 25 September 1864, stated that:

'The badge of the Twenty-third Corps is an escutcheon in the form of the heraldic shield, all of whose proportions are determined by the width, as follows: The sides of the shield are straight from the top for the distance of one-fourth the width of the shield. Each curved side is struck with the center at the lower point of the straight part of the opposite side and with a radius equal to the width . . .

'The flags of the corps are as follows: For corps headquarters, a blue flag with a shield in the center of

Although this Army of the Potomac headquarters flag would appear to be that of the 2d Division, I Corps, with a white disc on a blue field, there is no explanation for it being in the headquarters of Brigadier-General Samuel W. Crawford, who commanded the 3d Division, V Corps when this photograph was taken in 1864. The old I Corps merged into the 2d and 4th Divisions, V Corps, in March 1864. (US Army Military History Institute)

the form prescribed; the body of the shield divided into three panels, one panel at each principal angle of the shield; the upper left-hand panel red, the upper right-hand panel white, the lower panel blue, the whole surrounded by a gold outline one-twelfth as wide as the shield. For headquarters Second Division, the whole of the interior of the shield white, otherwise the same as the corps flag. For headquarters Third Division, the whole of the interior of the shield blue, otherwise the same as the corps flag. For brigade headquarters, a flag similar to the division flag, but with smaller shields along the inner margin

corresponding in number to the brigade. The artillery will wear the badge of the division to which the different batteries are respectively attached.'

According to one of its members, Major-General Jacob D. Cox, writing in 1887, the system of corps-wide flags lasted throughout the corps' existence. 'The *Corps Headquarters* flag was a silk banner of dark Army blue color, with gold fringe, and the corps badge emblazoned in the center. The Division Headquarters flags were, *1st Division*, Blue silk banner, yellow worsted fringe, the shield with the same shape as the corps shield in outline & panels, but the panels red in the gold outline. *2d Division*, Similar to the last with all the panels white. *3d Division*, Similar to last, with all the panels blue. The 3d Div. flag shows only the gold frame of the shield, the panels being of the same blue silk as the flag.

'The *Brigade Headquarters* flags were of blue bunting without any fringe. They were of the same

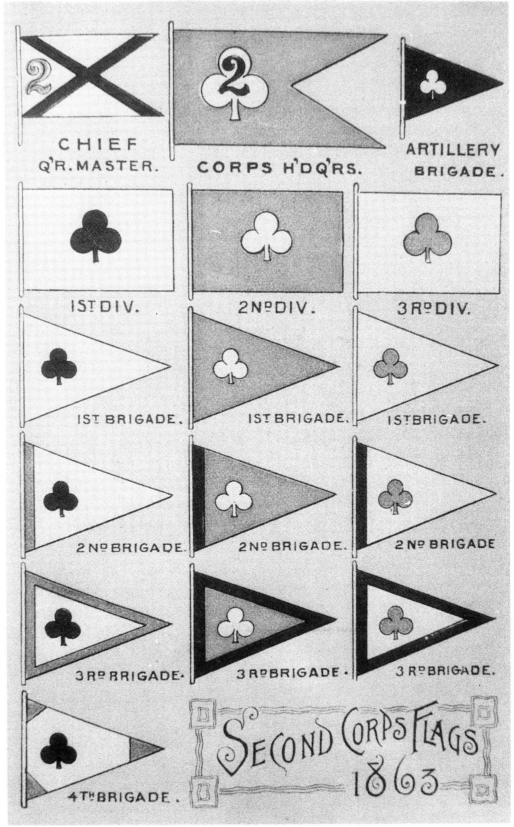

The headquarters flags of the II Corps in 1863. (Billings, Hard-tack and Coffee)

CHIEF
Q'R. MASTER.

CORPS H'DQ'RS.

ARTILLERY
BRIGADE.

1ST DIV.

2ND DIV.

3RD DIV.

1ST BRIGADE.

1ST BRIGADE.

1ST BRIGADE.

2ND BRIGADE.

2ND BRIGADE.

2ND BRIGADE

3RD BRIGADE.

3RD BRIGADE.

3RD BRIGADE.

4TH BRIGADE.

SECOND CORPS FLAGS
1863

style of shield as the division flags, but the shield smaller, & instead of being placed in the center of the flag, as many shields used indicated the number of the brigade, and they were placed in the corner of the flag where the Union Jack [*sic*] is in the National flag: Shields: 1st Div. Yellow frame, red panels; 2d Div. Yellow frame, white panels; 3d Div. Yellow frame, blue panels. The yellow frame of the shields on the brigade flags was usually made by tenacious yellow paint, the panels being of the red, white, or blue bunting, inserted in the blue flag.'

Third Division, Department of West Virginia

According to General Orders No. 7, issued 23 March 1864 by the headquarters, Third Division, Department of West Virginia: 'I. Hereafter flags will be used to designate the different headquarters of this division, as follows.

'For the division: A three-striped red, white, and blue flag—the stripes to be of width, running diagonally from top to bottom—red at top and white in center, five feet on the staff and six feet fly. The division to be designated by three blue stars thirteen inches long on the white field, the inner corner of which to be five and one-half inches from the staff.

'The brigade flags will be the same as that of the division, with the number of the Brigade in white, six inches long, in the center of each star. These flags to be attached to portable staffs twelve feet long, in two joints, and in the field will be displayed at the quarters of the officers whose headquarters it is intended to designate, and on the march, will be carried near that person.'

Major-General Winfield Scott Hancock, wearing a hat and with one hand on the tree, stands in front of the headquarters flags of the II Corps, the blue swallow-tail flag and a smaller national colour. (US Army Military History Institute)

CAVALRY FLAGS

This 1864 drawing shows two III Corps headquarters flags, that of the corps headquarters and the white flag with either a red lozenge for the 1st Division or a blue lozenge for the 3d Division.

Originally, Union forces divided cavalry units up among corps, which were largely infantry with artillery support. However, combat soon taught them that cavalry was best used independently; and each army soon adopted cavalry corps, marked by their own flags.

According to General Orders No. 119, 30 April 1862, in the Army of the Potomac, the Cavalry Reserve headquarters was to have a yellow rectangular flag with a blue St. Andrew's cross; the 1st Brigade, a blue star; and the 2d Brigade, two stars. General Orders No. 53, 12 May 1863, gave a yellow swallow-tailed guidon with white crossed sabres to the Cavalry Corps headquarters. Its formations used guidons of their own design, although most were made in the regulation horizontally halved form, red over white, with the division number in the opposite colour on each bar. Other units divided their guidons into three triangles—white on the hoist, blue on the top, and red on the bottom. A pair of crossed sabres was applied to the white triangle, while gold stars were often painted in the other two.

On 1 August 1864 a full system of Army of the Potomac Cavalry Corps colours was approved. It was very smilar to those used by the Army's other corps, with crossed sabres substituted for the corps badges,

Battle honours were often placed on headquarters flags as well as unit flags, although this was not strictly according to orders. This photograph of Major-General David B. Birney, who commanded the 1st Division, III Corps (bottom, centre, with two medals on his chest) shows both the corps headquarters flag and the division headquarters flag. The latter has battle honours, one for Chancellorsville to the right of the lozenge, painted on it in scrolls. (US Army Military History Institute)

complete with a dark blue swallow-tailed guidon for the corps headquarters, white and blue rectangular flags for the division headquarters, and pointed guidons for brigades.

On 26 April 1864 General Orders No. 62, Department of the Cumberland, prescribed a system of flags for its cavalry corps. The corps headquarters had a red, white, and blue flag similar to the French tricolour, with a large pair of gold crossed sabres extending over all three bars, and fringed in gold. The first and third divisions had white rectangular flags, the first with red crossed sabres and a blue number 1, the third with blue crossed sabres and a red number 3. The second division had a blue flag with white crossed sabres and a red number 2. Brigades received guidons generally following the Army of the Potomac corps flag system.

General Orders No. 3, 24 March 1864, in the Cavalry Corps, Military Division of the Mississippi, produced a different system of flags for that corps' seven divisions. All of its formations had swallow-tail guidons, that for the headquarters being red with yellow crossed sabres, while the divisions had white guidons with dark blue crossed sabres and the division number in red both above and below the sabres.

NAVAL FLAGS

Each commissioned ship of the US Navy and US Marine Revenue Cutter Service flew several flags. A jack, which was simply the dark blue canton with its white stars of the National Flag, was flown at the jack staff of the vessel's bow. A National Flag was flown from different staffs, according to the type of vessel; and a commission pennant identified the ship as a vessel of war. This was a long narrow flag, of blue with a line of white stars at the hoist, and two stripes, red above white.

Captains in command of squadrons, and later admirals, were entitled to fly (or 'wear' as it was then termed) a plain blue flag with as many white stars as there were states. In the case of several squadrons merging, the senior officer would use the blue flag while the next in rank had a red flag. If there was a third captain commanding a squadron in the group, he was entitled to fly the same flag in white.

In February 1865 the admiral's flag was changed from square to rectangular.

A contemporary illustration of the V Corps headquarters flag and one of its division headquarters flags. The headquarters flag marked with the backwards 'C' is probably intended to have a '6' for the VI Corps.

THE PLATES

A1: National Colour, 3d US Infantry Regiment, 1861

The national colour carried by the country's oldest continuously serving infantry regiment, the 3d, was made under federal contract through the Philadelphia Depot. It displays one of three known patterns of stars in its canton. The lower star is missing from the lower ring in the 34-star variety, while the 35-star variety has no central star but has 21 stars in the outer ring.

A2: National Colour, 1st Battalion, 11th US Infantry Regiment, 1863

This is a Tiffany & Company, New York, presentation national colour with typical script-embroidered

Brigadier-General Charles Griffin (standing with open coat and slouch hat) commanded the I Division, V Corps, in late 1863 when this photograph was taken. The *headquarters flag is white with a red Maltese cross. (US Army Military History Institute)*

unit designation and battle honours. According to tradition, this colour was presented on 22 February 1862; the battle honour for Gettysburg (1–3 July 1863) would indicate that this is incorrect. Apparently the 11th through 19th US Infantry Regiments, which had three battalions, issued regimental colours for their first two battalions, which usually served apart (although probably also to their third battalions, which served as depots if, as few were, they were even organized).

A3: Regimental Colour, 6th US Infantry Regiment, 1863

The 6th Infantry's regimental colour was a Cincin-nati Depot federal contract model, believed made by John Shilleto of that city. He received orders for five infantry regimental, two artillery regimental and five national colours on 3 November 1862. Some varieties of these flags have different numbers of stars, yet all have an upper arc that overlaps the end of the motto scroll.

B1: Regimental Colour, 164th New York Infantry Regiment, 1864

This flag was supplied under a New York Depot federal contract. Similar colours display 34 stars; these have only 16 stars in the lower arc.

B2: Standard, 2d US Cavalry Regiment, 1861

Cavalry standards were smaller than those carried by foot regiments for two reasons: there was not as much need for unit identification of mounted units on the field as for foot units; and, the larger the flag, the more difficult it was to carry on the march or in action.

B3: Regimental Colour, 5th US Artillery Regiment, 1862

Cords and tassels on artillery colours were red and yellow intermixed silk, and crossed cannon replaced the national eagle shown on infantry colours. The colours were also the same size for both infantry and artillery regiments.

B4: Regimental Colour, artillery, 1864

In 1863 the design on the artillery regimental colour was enlarged to fill more of the field. This particular colour was made under a New York Depot federal contract. Often partially decorated scrolls were placed on a colour issued to a regiment, which would then be responsible for having the number filled in. This was true of infantry as well as artillery colours.

C1: Designating flag, 1st Brigade, 2d Division of a Corps; Army of the Potomac, 1862

Under the 1862 system of designating flags issued in the Army of the Potomac, each first brigade of a second division, regardless of corps, was to carry this blue and white flag, which measured 5 ft. by 6 ft. This actual flag is in the collection of the US Army Military Academy Museum, West Point, New York. It measures 58 inches at the hoist by 72 inches in the fly.

C2: Designating flag, 3d Brigade, 1st Division of a Corps, Army of the Potomac, 1862

This is another surviving example of an 1862 Army of the Potomac designating flag. This one, which measures 60 inches by 72 inches, is in the New York State Collection.

C3: Designating flag, 1st Brigade, 4th Division of a Corps; Army of the Potomac, 1862

This designating flag, now in the West Point collection, was probably carried in Ord's Division of the Department of the Rappahannock. It measures 54 inches by 70 inches.

This sketch shows the 1st Division, V Corps headquarters flag being carried into battle at Preble's Farm, Virginia, on 30 September 1864.

This photograph of X Corps commander Major-General Alfred H. Terry (in the coat with two rows of buttons arranged in threes) shows the standard Army of the Potomac corps headquarters flag being used in that corps instead of the rectangular blue flag bearing a plain number 10 as ordered in the Army of the James. (National Archives)

C4: Designating flag, 11th Pennsylvania Volunteer Infantry Regiment, 1862

The colours and number on this flag indicate that the unit that carried it was the fourth regiment of the third brigade of the second division, of the III Corps of the Army of the Potomac. In this case, the regiment was the 11th Pennsylvania, which carried this flag in the Second Battle of Manassas.

D1: Headquarters, I Corps, 1863

On 7 February 1863, under General Orders No. 10, all corps headquarters in the Army of the Potomac were to have blue swallow-tailed guidons with a white 'Maltese cross' bearing the corps number in red. This odd device, which is not a true Maltese cross by any means, became the standard symbol used. It is

actually a cross *botonée*, that is a Greek cross with a trefoil bud at the end of each arm.

D2: 3d Brigade, 2d Division, I Corps, 1863

The Army of the Potomac system of identifying flags adopted on 7 February 1863 gave corps headquarters a swallow-tailed guidon, with a rectangular flag carried by each division headquarters, and this type of guidon by each brigade headquarters. The white circle is the I Corps badge, which was also worn on soldiers' and officers' headgear and, at times, on the left breast. On 1 August 1864 the corps badge was authorized by General Orders No. 115 to be used on all corps flags.

D3: Headquarters, II Corps, 1864

On 1 August 1864, General Orders No. 115 changed the II Corps headquarters flag by using the assigned Corps badge, a 'trefoil', in place of the 'Maltese cross'. The same device appeared on all this corps' flags, in red for the first division, white for the second division, and blue for the third division. The artillery brigade had a red guidon with a white trefoil, while the corps chief quartermaster had a dark blue swallow-tail guidon with a St. Andrew's cross in white.

D4: 3d Division, III Corps, 1864

Under the system of 1 August 1864, all 3d Division, III Corps flags used a blue corps badge, the lozenge; the 1st and 3d Divisions' headquarters had white flags (with a red lozenge for the 1st Division), whilst the 2d Division headquarters had a blue flag with a white lozenge. The brigade guidons matched the colours, with the first brigade having plain white, the second having a red stripe at the hoist, the third being bordered in red, and the fourth with red tips. Actually III Corps had been merged into II Corps by the time these flags were ordered, although many did see use until the system was changed by Special Orders No. 320, issued 24 November 1864. The flag of the 3d Division under those orders, now in the New Jersey State Capital, has a white background with a blue trefoil within a red lozenge on the field.

E1: 2d Division, V Corps, 1864

The corps badge of the Army of the Potomac's V Corps was the Maltese cross, which appears in white on its 2d Division's headquarters flag. The V Corps received elements of the old I Corps as the V Corps' 2d and 4th Divisions on 24 March 1864. The old I Corps units were allowed to keep their old corps badges and unit flags; on 11 September 1864 all the I Corps elements were further reduced to the 3d Division, V Corps, complete with their old insignia. On 20 December 1864 a circular ordered all men of the division to wear a 'White Maltese Cross' on their hats and all elements of the old I Corps badges were done away with.

E2: 1st Division, VI Corps, 1864

Although originally the Greek cross worn by the VI Corps was ordered to be worn 'upright', it appeared as a St. Andrew's cross on a number of headquarters flags carried within the Corps starting in 1864. The Greek cross was carried in the 3d Division; the other divisions used the St. Andrew's cross.

E3: Headquarters, IX Corps, 1864

The IX Corps adopted this unusual corps badge,

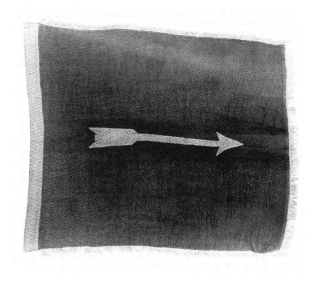

This headquarters flag, in blue with a red arrow and yellow fringe, measures $3\frac{1}{2}$ by $4\frac{1}{2}$ ft., and identified the 1st Division, XVII Corps in 1865. (West Point Museum Collections)

signifying its service as a landing force along the south-eastern coast, on 10 April 1864. The first Corps headquarters flag used the Army of the Potomac's 'Maltese cross' design with a red number 9; it was replaced by a national flag with a corps badge in the canton, surrounded by an oval of stars, in April 1864. This flag was adopted when the Corps was attached to the Army of the Potomac in May 1864, although one source says it was not adopted until 1 August 1864. The divisional flags were red (1st Division), white (2d Division), blue (3d Division), and green (4th Division) with a corps badge of a facing colour. Rectangular brigade flags had three vertical stripes with a corps badge and brigade number.

E4: Headquarters, X Corps, 1864

On 3 May 1864 the X Corps adopted square flags for its headquarters and division headquarters. While the number 10 was used on the corps headquarters flags, the divisions had one, two, and three white stars respectively on their blue flags. On 22 May 1864 the Corps' commander wrote: 'I have received four flags. I propose to replace the stars on the division flags by the corps badge, which is a square bastioned fort, very like a star in effect, I presume there can be no objection to this.' There has been no reply found and, moreover, photographs show the older flag with number 10 in use until the corps' demise in December 1864. Photographs of the recreated corps headquarters, taken after March 1865, show the Army of the Potomac's blue swallowtail guidon with white 'Maltese cross' and red number 10 being used.

F1: Headquarters, XXIV Corps, 1865

The corps badge of the XXIV Corps, Department of Virginia, created from elements of the old X and XVIII Corps, was adopted on 1 March 1865. It consisted of the corps number in red within a white

(Left) *The flag carried by the Chief Quartermaster, XIX Corps, in 1864–65 featured a red cross on a white disc on a blue field. It measures $2\frac{1}{2}$ by $3\frac{1}{2}$ ft. (West Point Museum Collections)*

(Right) *The headquarters flag of Brigadier-General Hugh Judson Kilpatrick (standing behind seated lady), who commanded cavalry in the Army of the Cumberland, had red and white stripes, with a white disc in the centre around an eagle mounted on a national colour in natural colours. The word 'TUEBOR' was painted in black. The photograph was taken in Stevensburg, Virginia, in March 1864 (US Army Military History Institute)*

There are some flags which were clearly made for unit identification but whose purpose is unknown today. This flag, for example, was found among the effects of Thomas Low of Tennessee, who served in the 2d US Tennessee Infantry, which was in the 7th Division in Alabama at one point. It appears to be some sort of identification flag for that unit, but no orders establishing its design have been found. It has a white field, with red stripes along the fly, and blue four-pointed stars, a blue eagle, and blue number 7. (Mike Miner Collection)

heart. The flag measures 36 inches at the hoist by 72 inches in the fly.

F2: Headquarters, XXIII Corps, 1864

Special Field Orders No. 121, dated 25 September 1864, of the XXIII Corps, Army of the Ohio, read: 'The flags of this corps are as follows: For corps headquarters, a blue flag with a shield in the corner of the form prescribed; the body of the shield divided into three panels, one panel at each principal angle of the shield; the upper left-hand panel red, the upper right-hand panel white, the lower panel blue, the whole surrounded by a golden outline one-twelfth as wide as the shield. For headquarters Second Division, the whole of the interior of the shield white, otherwise the same as the corps flag. For headquarters Third Division, the whole of the interior blue, otherwise the same as the corps flag. For brigade headquarters, a flag similar to the division flag, but with smaller shield along the inner margin corres-

ponding in number to the brigade. The artillery will wear the badge of the division to which the different batteries are respectively attached.' The 1st Division presumably received the same flag with a red shield on joining the corps in the spring of 1865.

F3: Headquarters, XV Corps, 1865

By General Orders No. 21, dated 9 April 1865, the XV Corps adopted its corps badge of a cartridge box under the motto 'FORTY ROUNDS' as the centrepiece of its flags. The rectangular flags carried by headquarters and division headquarters were 5 ft. by 5 ft. 6 ins. The division flags were all red for the 1st Division, white for the 2d, blue for the 3d, and yellow for the 4th; the corps headquarters flag was quartered in the three first division colours. Swallow-tailed guidons were carried by brigade headquarters. These measured 4 ft. by 5 ft. 6 ins. and came in appropriate division colours with different borders to designate the different brigades. The corps badges on surviving examples have been painted on the fields.

Major-General David M. Gregg (seated, wearing a slouch hat) commanded the 2d Division, Cavalry Corps, Army of the Potomac. The red and white division

headquarters flag is tied to his tent pole. (US Army Military History Institute)

ters flag using this device appears to have been taken into use around July 1864.

G1: 2d Division, XIX Corps, 1864

On 18 February 1863, XIX Corps, of the Department of the Gulf, issued its General Orders No. 17 which called for a headquarters flag: 'A blue flag with a white four-pointed star, in the center; the number 19, in red, on the star.' Each division flag was 'red, with a white four-pointed star, in the center, the number of the division in black figures on the star'. General Orders No. 11, 17 November 1864, revised the system to use the corps' newly adopted badge, 'a fan-leaved cross with octagonal center'. Headquarters used a blue swallow-tailed guidon with a white corps badge, while the guidon used by the 2d Division reversed the colours.

F4: 2d Division, XVIII Corps, 1864

The XVIII Corps, of the Army of the James, first adopted the same type of flags as used in the X Corps, with the corps number in white on the headquarters flag, and one, two, or three stars, according to the division, on each division headquarters flag. Instead of the blue fields of the X Corps, the XVIII Corps used red. However, on 7 June 1864 a 'cross with foliate sides', similar to the 'Maltese cross' used on Army of the Potomac corps headquarters flags, was adopted as the corps badge. A new corps headquar-

G2: Headquarters, XX Corps, 1864

The XX Corps of the Army of the Cumberland was formed on 4 April 1864 from units of the XXII Corps and the XXI Corps. On 26 April Department of the Cumberland General Orders No. 62 awarded its headquarters a blue swallow-tailed guidon with a white 'Tunic cross' and the red number 20. Old XXII Corps flags were used by the division head-quarters, with a 6 ft. square white flag with a blue star in the 3d Division, and a red field with a green star in the 4th Division. Triangular flags, each side being 6 ft. long, were used by brigade headquarters; these followed the Army of the Potomac system for differentiating brigades.

G3: Headquarters, IV Corps, Army of the Cumberland, 1864

The IV Corps of the Army of the Cumberland was different from most corps in that its badge, an equilateral triangle, was not used in any form on the corps flags. Instead, corps and division headquarters used red flags with a blue canton. Headquarters used a golden eagle in its canton.

G4: 3d Division, IV Corps, 1864

Each division of the IV Corps used white stripes to make a design in the blue cantons of their otherwise red flags. The 1st Division had one stripe running diagonally from bottom left to top right; the 2d had a white St. Andrew's cross; and the 3d, a white St. Andrew's cross with a vertical stripe through the middle. Brigades had swallow-tailed guidons with the same canton as their division, but with one, two, or three white stars under the canton according to the brigade number.

H1: Co. I, 6th Pennsylvania Cavalry (Rush's Lancers), 1863

This regulation cavalry guidon was carried by the cavalry company that accompanied the headquarters of the Army of the Potomac during the Battle of Gettysburg. The battle honour for that engagement would therefore suggest that it was carried for some time at least after July 1863. The cavalryman holding the guidon wears the dress jacket worn by mounted troops, trimmed in yellow for cavalry.

H2: Headquarters, XXI Corps, 1863

The oddly-shaped XXI Corps flags were prescribed in the Department of the Cumberland's General Orders No. 91, 25 April 1863. The corps headquarters flag, which was 6 ft. in hoist by 4 ft. in the fly, used an eagle with the number 21, while divisions had from one to three stars on the white stripe. Brigades used the division flags, but with the white number of the brigade replacing the star.

H3: Headquarters, Cavalry Corps, Army of the Potomac, 1864

Cavalry in the Army of the Potomac used a variety of systems of flag identification, starting from 1862 when a blue St. Andrew's cross on a yellow field was authorized for the cavalry reserve headquarters. On 12 May 1863 it was authorized a yellow swallow-tailed flag with white crossed sabres in the centre. Thereafter most cavalry commands used crossed sabres, the traditional Cavalry Corps badge, on their flags. This headquarters flag was adopted in 1864 and apparently used until the end of the war.

INTRODUCTION

Most Civil War soldiers, although they served in a national Union or Confederate Army, fought under a state designation—eg. the 72st Pennsylvania Volunteer Infantry Regiment, 27th Volunteer Virginia Infantry Regiment, etc.—and often felt that they were representing their state as much as their country. So it was only natural that many carried state flags, or national flags with state seals and mottos, as their regimental colours. Indeed, for a time many Confederate troops were ordered to carry state flags since the Confederate first national flag was so

Seals of the state. These were commonly used on state flags.

like the US national flag that commanders were often confused by the two in the smoke of battle (see pages 15-20 earlier in this volume).

A number of units, especially in the more well-to-do Union Army where time and money was available for special extras, carried unique flags which violated their army regulations:

'On May 10 a number of men from Cincinnati, on behalf of Cincinnati's German women, had come to give us a flag. Thirteen gold stars rode in a field of blue silk above a pennant inscribed, on one side, "To Cincinnati's first German regiment," and on the other, "Fight bravely for Freedom and Justice,"' reported the historian of the 9th Ohio Infantry Regiment. 'The colors were the result of one-day's effort by the Misses Elise Arnold and Karoline Greslin. With words of pure patriotism, Dr. Bauer

handed the colors to the colonel, who accepted them for the regiment and pledged his sincere intent that they be carried ever forward to victory and to German honor. Sergeant Fitz, named standard-bearer then and there, received the beautiful colors with appropriate dignity.'

Before the Civil War the United States had a flourishing network of uniformed volunteer militia units in addition to the common militia, which was made up of virtually the whole male population. Uniformed volunteer units were raised by individuals, usually from an area's social élite who had enough spare money and time to spend on such enthusiasms. They voted on their unit designation, their officers, and non-commissioned officers, their unit rules, and their uniform. A unit could apply to its state to be taken on to the militia muster rolls, which meant that the state would supply its weapons. Not all states had a militia system, however, and some units preferred independence anyway. A number of both types of unit survive today in state National Guard or as state-chartered units.

The uniformed units were generally most noted for their 'fancy dress'; but they did also help to bring the country closer together – they spent a great deal of time visiting each other's towns and participating in joint drills and parades. Many future leaders learned their skills in these ranks, and volunteer militia units formed the core of many fighting units on both sides of the Mason-Dixon line. Counting both sides, there were thousands of volunteer units in existence.

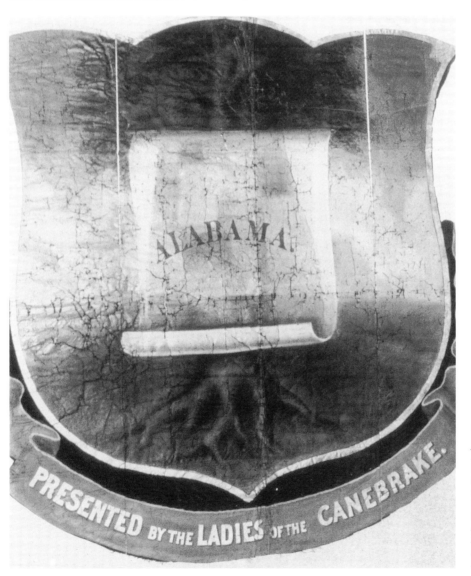

The device on the flag presented to the Cane brake Rifle Guards in 1861 was the map of Alabama superimposed on a tree, used as a state seal since the 1850s. The company was later designated Co.D, 4th Alabama Infantry Regiment. (State of Alabama, Department of Archives and History)

The flag presented to the Claiborne Guards in March 1861 was similar to the Confederate first national flag, save that it had only seven bars and stars, as well as having the company designation in the canton. The company later became Co.C, 2d Alabama Infantry Regiment. (State of Alabama, Department of Archives and History)

Alabama

When Alabama officially left the Union on 11 January 1861 the state did not have a regulation flag. However, some of the leading women of the state's capital city of Montgomery had previously prepared a flag for the occasion, and this was flown over the capital building for the first time at that date. It became the state's official flag thereafter.

It was novel for a state flag in that the obverse and reverse had different designs. Both sides had a blue field. The obverse featured the goddess Liberty wearing a red gown and holding a sword in her right hand, and a blue flag bearing a yellow five-pointed star—a version of the 'bonnie blue flag'—in her left hand. The state name ALABAMA in yellow letters appeared over the star on the smaller flag. Above the goddess was the motto INDEPENDENT NOW AND FOREVER.

The design on the reverse featured a cotton plant guarded by a rattlesnake over the motto NOLI ME TANGERE ('Do not touch me'), a design made popular during the War of American Independence.

This elaborate flag saw little if any military use. Almost immediately a simpler version appeared, featuring a blue field with a yellow five-pointed star. At times the star appeared under the word ALABAMA, and sometimes also with the goddess Liberty.

None of these designs appear to have been used much either by Alabama's first volunteer units, who usually carried flags of their own design, sometimes with the state map (which also appeared on state-issued buckles and buttons), or by units formed after the state joined the Confederacy in February 1861.

Arkansas

Arkansas had no official state flag; in keeping, however, with standard practices, the state seal may have been painted on some early flags. In the seal, according to Wells' *The National Handbook*, 'Occupying the lower part of a circle is a shield, near the base of which is a white star on a blue field, representing the State. In the middle portion is a bee hive, signifying industry, and a plough, denoting agriculture; while a steamboat, emblematic of commerce, fills the upper part. For the crest, the goddess of liberty is represented with her wand and cap in one hand, and a wreath of laurel in the other, surrounded by a constellation of stars, indicating the States. The supporters [are] two eagles, one grasping a bundle of arrows, and the other an olive branch; a label extending from the claw of each, with the motto *Regnant Populi*—"The People rule." On either side of the base is a cornucopia. . . .'

Connecticut

Connecticut's pre-war militia apparently carried both a standard national color, and a dark blue

The flag of the 58th Regiment, Massachusetts Volunteer Infantry Regiment (Third Veteran), was captured at the Battle of the Crater, where the regiment lost 172 of 200 men engaged. It is white and has four ties. (Massachusetts State House, Bureau of State Office Buildings)

regimental color which bore the painted state seal and the regimental designation under it. Such flags were carried by the state's troops as early as 1775. In 1861 the state legislature almost adopted a white version of the regimental color as a state flag, but the passage of the bill was postponed in the state House of Representatives.

As a result, most of the state's infantry regiments carried dark blue regimental colors with an eagle over the state seal of three vines on a white field within an elaborate scroll shadowed by a national red, white, and blue shield. The regimental designation was printed in blue Roman capital letters on a gold scroll under the seal. However, the 1st Connecticut Infantry had this flag in white; and the 9th Infantry had this flag with a golden harp on a green device in place of the three vines along with the shield. The beautiful presentation flag of the 13th Infantry, which was made by Tiffany & Co., New York, had a symmetrical state seal under an eagle about to take off, with the state motto in gold-embroidered letters under the seal and the regimental designation above the eagle. Battle honours were embroidered in script

on the bottom half of the flag. The 27th Infantry carried a regulation US infantry regimental color.

According to *The National Handbook*, 'The original seal is of an oval form, without any ornamental devices, and on the field are delineated three grape-vines, each winding around and sustained by an upright support, the whole representing the three settlements (Hartford, Windsor, and Wethersfield) which formed the early colony.'

Connecticut regiments' national colors often had an eagle painted or embroidered in their cantons. Battle honours were often painted on these colors, although streamers were issued to the 5th and 14th Connecticut Infantry Regiments by 1864.

Delaware

Although Delaware had no official state flag, some of its units apparently used the state seal on a dark blue field. The 1st Delaware Infantry Regiment's regimental color included the state seal, although the other regiments appear to have used regulation US Army colors.

According to *The National Handbook*, the state

seal featured 'An azure shield, or escutcheon, divided into two equal parts by a white band or girdle. A cow is represented in the lower part of the shield, and in the upper part are two symbols, designed probably to represent the agricultural production of the State—grain and tobacco. The crest [a wreath] supports a ship under full sail, displaying the American banner. On a white field around the escutcheon were formally wreaths of flowers, branches of the olive, and other symbols, but these have been displaced for [by] two figures, representing a mariner and a hunter.'

The flag of the 1st had a blue riband over the seal bearing the words LIBERTY AND INDE-PENDENCE in gold, and a red riband under the seal with the regimental designation, also in gold.

Florida

When Florida left the Union on 10 January 1861 she did not have a state flag. Improvising, the first Florida troops used flags which bore a single star. The Military Department of the State went ahead and ordered a flag that featured 13 alternating red and white stripes, with a blue canton bearing a single five-pointed white star in its centre, on 13 January 1861. This flag was first flown over the navy yard at Pensacola the following day.

On 8 February the legislature instructed the state's governor to design an official state flag. He obviously had more urgent matters on his mind, since his executive order describing the state's new flag was not issued until 13 September 1861. This flag was essentially the Confederate first national color, with the canton extended to run the full length of the hoist as a vertical bar. Within the canton was the state's new seal in an oval surrounded by the motto in Roman letters over the seal's top, IN GOD IS OUR TRUST, and the name of the state below the seal. The seal itself featured several stands of arms, a cannon, a drum, cannon balls, and two flags—one a Confederate first national flag—beneath a live oak tree, with several ships at sea in the background. This scene was painted in natural colours.

Although on 4 December 1863 the legislature ordered the governor to provide 'each regiment and battalion in Confederate service from this state a suitable flag or ensign', the flags issued to the state's troops appear to have been various copies of the Army of Northern Virginia battle flags rather than state flags.

Georgia

When Georgia seceded on 19 January 1861 a new flag was flown over the state's capital at Milledgeville. It was described as having the state's seal on a white field; however, traditionally a blue field was used, while a surviving state flag in the Museum of the

The governor of the Commonwealth of Massachusetts presents a typical white state flag to the 12th Massachusetts Infantry Regiment in 1861. Note the elaborate tassels.

Confederacy has a red field. The red flag, with a five-pointed white star in the centre, had been flown by the Augusta Battalion in 1861 when it took over the Augusta Arsenal.

According to Wells' *Handbook*, in the seal, 'In the centre of a circular white or silver field are three pillars, supporting an arch, around which are emblazoned the word "Constitution." The pillars are symbolic of the three departments of the State government—the Legislative, the Judiciary, and the Executive: and on the one on the right, representing the Legislative, is the word "Wisdom;" on the second, representing the Judiciary, is the word "Justice:" and on the third, representing the Executive, is the word "Moderation." Near the right pillar is the figure of an officer with a drawn sword, denoting that the aid of the military is always ready to enforce respect and obedience to law.'

In at least one surviving example the state seal is painted on a blue field in natural colours with seven gold five-pointed stars, the centre one slightly larger than the others, with the bottom points just touching the bottom of the painted state seal. The riband hanging from the white temple pillars is red with yellow lettering; the soldier stands to the far left.

The state seal was used in the canton of a silk Confederate first national flag, within a ring of 11 white stars, by an unknown Georgia unit. This may have been common among the state's first troops. Otherwise, Georgia units apparently carried regulation army colors in the field. Indeed, the state's governor apparently flew a version of the Army of Northern Virginia battle flag over his headquarters.

Illinois

Illinois did not have a state flag until 1915, its troops apparently using regulation army colors. Indeed, the state's adjutant general wrote in 1879, 'The devices upon the regimental colors of the State militia have varied with the taste of their donors, or at the caprice of the regimental officers.' Surviving state unit flags appear largely to have conformed to US Army regulations.

Indiana

Although it is generally believed that most Indiana regiments carried regulation flags, at least the 13th Indiana Infantry Regiment carried a dark blue regimental color with the state seal embroidered in natural colours in the centre over a small red, white,

The centre of the flag of the 1st Regiment, Massachusetts Heavy Artillery, was torn by a 30-pound shell at the Battle of Sailor's Creek, Virginia, 6 April 1865. (Massachusetts State House, Bureau of State Office Buildings)

and blue US shield, over a red scroll with the motto *E Pluribue Unum* in blue letters. The regimental designation was printed in gold Roman letters on a red riband over the seal (13th. REGt. INDIANA VOLs.), while a battle honour for Rich Mountain was placed in a similar scroll beneath the seal. Another honour (WINCHESTER/23rd. March 1862) was placed where the canton would normally be. The whole flag was fringed with gold.

The seal is described thus by Wells: 'In the lower portion of a circular field is represented a scene of prairie and woodland, with the surface gently undulating—descriptive of the predominant features of the State. In the foreground is a buffalo, an animal once abounding in great numbers in this region, apparently startled by the axe of the woodman or pioneeer, who is seen on the left, felling the trees of the forest, denoting the march of civilization westward. In the distance, on the right, is seen the sun, just appearing above the verge of the horizon.'

Iowa-Kansas

The story about Iowa's and Kansas' flags is the same as that of Illinois—there was no state flag, and the state's troops apparently mostly carried regulation US Army colors. Kansas, being a divided state, had men fighting for both sides; those for the South often had flags marked SOUTHERN RIGHTS, while those for the North had flags inscribed OUR LIVES FOR OUR RIGHTS.

Kentucky

While there was no official state flag during the period, in 1866 the state's adjutant general wrote that Union units often carried colors made to regulation US Army regimental color size, of light blue silk with a blue fringed border; the state seal was painted in its centre. Indeed, a dark blue version of this flag became the official state National Guard flag in 1880. This would match the 1860 state militia laws, which required: 'Each regiment shall be provided with a color, which shall be that of the United States, with the arms of the State of Kentucky and the number of the regiment painted or embroidered there on.'

On 4 December 1861, the state's quartermaster general wrote to the supplier of the state's flag, Hugh Wilkins of Louisville: 'Our law requires that the coat of arms of the state of Kentucky shall be centered on

The battle-torn colors of the 19th Massachusetts Infantry, including the state flag on the right, had axeheads on their top. (US Army Military History Institute)

the regimental color. The nationality of the regiment is sufficiently displayed by the stars and stripes. You will therefore paint the name of the state alone on the regimental color.'

The state seal showed, according to Wells' *Handbook*: 'In the centre of a circular white or silver field, two friends are seen grasping one hand of each other in a firm and cordial embrace, while the other is extended to each other's back, significant of encouragement and support. Below them is the expressive motto, "United we stand; divided we fall."'

In the actual seal, as painted on Wilkins' flags, the figure on the left looks like George Washington, with white hair and blue and buff 1790s period dress, while that on the right wears frontier garb of a fringed buckskin shirt and trousers and a coonskin cap, and holds a rifle. What appears to be water can be seen

behind the right-hand figure, and several trees behind the man on the right. The motto is painted in gold capital letters on a red riband over the oval seal, which has scalloped edges, while the unit designation, e.g. 13TH REGT. KY. VOL. INF., is painted in the same type of letters on a red riband under the seal.

These state regimental colors made by Wilkins are known to have been issued to the 1st, 2d, 3d, 9th, 10th, 11th, 12th, 13th, 14th, 16th, 18th, 20th, 24th, and 27th Kentucky Volunteer Infantry Regiments. The 15th Infantry carried a local presentation color, as apparently did the 25th Infantry. Other regiments may have received regulation US Army regimental colors provided by the Army.

A pre-war flag carried by the Woodford Blues, a Kentucky State Guard company from Versaillers, Woodford County, was of dark blue silk, four feet by seven feet. However, instead of the state seal it bore in its centre a Union eagle within a circle, with 13 five-pointed white stars around the circle and a wreath underneath it with the letters K.S.G. directly under the eagle. A red scroll bears the unit designation WOODFORD BLUES below that. The company largely joined the Confederate Kentucky Brigade. However, most Confederate Kentucky flags known

today appear to be variations of regulation national or battle flags.

Louisiana

The earliest state flag, raised on receipt of the news of South Carolina's secession in December 1860, featured a red field with a single five-pointed white star in its centre, with a pelican feeding its young in a nest painted within the star. The pelican had long been a state symbol, appearing on the flags of troops raised in the state as early as the Mexican-American War of 1846–48.

However, this familiar device was abandoned when the state chose an official flag on 11 February 1861. This flag was similar to the old US flag, with stripes of blue, white, and red, and a blue canton. A single yellow five-pointed star, symbolic of the state standing alone, was placed in the centre of the canton.

Despite this official flag, which remained the state flag until the end of the war, the pelican remained the most common device on state flags. In May 1862, when the state's capital city of Baton Rouge fell to Union troops, the flag found flying over the state capitol had a blue field with a single star with the pelican device painted in its centre. By 1864 Confederate versions of this flag often had the word

JUSTICE painted under the pelican's nest; when Union troops were raised in the state, the motto was more often UNION.

Maine

Like other Union states, Maine had no official state flag in 1861, but often issued flags with the state seal painted on a dark blue field, of US Army regimental color size. Such a flag was carried by e.g. the 11th Maine Infantry, also bearing 26 battle honours such

The colors of the 15th New York Engineers. The regimental color bears the state seal. (National Archives)

as 'Siege of Charleston, S.C. (Swamp Angle)', 'Night attack on Beauregard's Train', 'Strawberry Plains (5 days)', and finally, '26th Appomattox Court House'.

According to Wells' *Handbook* the seal featured 'A white or silver shield, on which is represented a pine-tree, with a moose-deer recumbent at its base—emblematical of the valuable timber of the State, and of the security and repose enjoyed by the animals which range its immense forests. The "supporters" are a mariner resting on his anchor, and a husbandman with his scythe—denoting that commerce and agriculture are each primary resources of the State. Above the shield is the North Star, beneath which is the motto, *Dirigo*—"I direct;" and under the shield is

the name of the State, in Roman capitals; while sea and land comprise the foreground. On the left, the tall masts of a ship are perceptible in the distance, the sails spread, denoting a readiness for commercial enterprise.'

Maryland

Maryland had no regulation state flag. Both Union and Confederate troops often carried dark blue flags with the state seal painted in the centre, although most units also carried their army's regulation colors. Indeed, the blue flag became the state's official flag in 1866.

There were two state seals at the time. One featured the figure of Justice grasping an olive branch, and a sword in her right hand, with a laurel wreath, tobacco, and ships around her. This does not appear on state military equipment. Indeed, the seal adopted in 1854, based on that used by the state's founder Lord Baltimore, was more commonly used as the state insignia. It featured a shield in the centre, quartered, with six vertical strips of yellow and black with a countercharged diagonal on the top left and bottom right, and white and red quarters with a countercharged cross *botonée* (with 'buttons' at the end of the arms) on the other two quarters. A 17th century sailor stood on the right of the shield, and a

soldier on the left. Above them was an eagle resting on a vase. The motto CRESCITE ET MULTIPLICAMINI was placed on a riband under the whole.

With the defeat of the Union 42d Pennsylvania Volunteer Infantry by the Confederate 1st Maryland Infantry, in June 1862 the Marylanders were authorised 'to have one of the captured "Bucktails"... appended to the color-staff of the 1st Maryland Regiment'—men of the 42d wore bucktails on their forage caps as a unit distinction.

The cross *botonée* also became a symbol of Maryland's Confederates. In 1863 the commander of the Maryland Line, a collection of Maryland units in Confederate service, ordered the officers and men of each regiment to wear 'a red cross on a ground of different colors, or something that way. But the failure to get the scraps of cloth from the factories prevented his carrying out this project.' Nonetheless, the Maryland Brigade headquarters was marked by a white swallow-tailed guidon with a narrow red border, and a red cross *botonée* in the centre.

Massachusetts

The well-established practice of the state's foot troops in the years just before the Civil War was to carry a white silk flag the size of a US Army

The Garibaldi Guards was a New York regiment raised from a mixture of European natives. The flag, seen hanging from the doorway, was red, white, and green, the Italian colours, with the letters GG on the centre stripe.

regimental flag with the state seal with a standing Indian painted in natural colours on the obverse, and the same design with a pine tree substituted for the Indian on the reverse. Mounted troops often carried flags of the style authorised for their branches of service with the same state seal and pine tree added. This practice continued into the war years, although, judging from surviving flags at the State House in Boston, about half of the state's regiments carried regulation colors, both national and regimental.

On the seal, according to Wells, 'On a blue ground of an irregularly-formed shield an Indian is represented, dressed with belted hunting-shirt and moccasins. In his right hand is a golden bow, and in his left an arrow with the point downward. A silver star on the right denotes one of the United States of America. A wreath forms the crest of the escutcheon, from which extends a right arm, clothed and ruffed, the hand grasping a broad-sword, the pommel and hilt of which are of gold. Around the escutcheon on a waving band or label, are the words, *Ense petit placidam sub libertate quietem*—"By the sword she seeks peace under liberty." '

Michigan

Michigan's state seal had been adopted in 1835, and a flag which incorporated the seal on its field was adopted in 1837. However, the official state flag, which had the state seal on the obverse and national arms on the reverse, first appeared on 4 July 1865 at a ceremony at the national cemetery at Gettysburg. The state seal on a blue flag served as an unofficial regimental color for a number of Michigan's infantry regiments even before then.

According to Wells, in the seal, 'On an escutcheon in the centre of a white field is the representative of a peninsula extending into a lake, a man with his gun, and a rising sun. On the upper part is the word *Tuebor*—"I will defend it"; and on a label extending across the lower part is the motto, *Si quarris peninsulam anaenam circumspice*—"If you seek a delightful country (peninsula), behold it." The supporters are a common deer on the right, and a moose on the left, both abounding in the forests of Michigan. For the crest is the American eagle; above which, on a label waving above all, is the motto, *E Pluribus Unum*.'

The 1st Michigan Infantry Regiment carried

A reconstruction of the color carried by the 11th New York Infantry (Fire Zouaves). It features equipment, such as a helmet, ladders, hooks, and axes, associated with fire fighting.

such a flag which was, according to the Roman capital letters on the red scroll above the seal, presented by MICHIGAN'S DAUGHTERS TO HER SONS DEFENDING IT. The regimental designation, 1ST. REGT. INFTY., is painted in gold letters on an almost black riband that hangs from the blue riband under the seal which bears the state motto.

Minnesota

Although Minnesota's adjutant-general wrote in 1880 that the state's troops did not carry state flags, the regimental color of the 5th Minnesota Infantry, at least, bore the state seal on one side and the national arms on the other. It is quite likely that other Minnesota regiments had similarly differenced flags.

According to Wells, 'The seal of this State represents the peculiar circumstances under which it was originally settled, when the white man first undertook to convert its comparative deserts into productive agricultural fields. In the distance, an Indian is seen mounted on a swift steed, retreating from the haunts where he had long been accustomed to enjoy unmolested the sports of the chase, and to roam uninterruptedly amidst his native forests. In the foreground is seen the new settler, preparing for his future subsistence by turning up the furrow, preparatory to sowing seed for the harvest. His gun and ammunition are lying behind him, ready to repel the assaults of the savage foes, to which he is constantly exposed. The motto, *L'Etoile du Nord*, (the Star of the North) is expressive of the bright future this State is destined to realize.'

Mississippi

On 26 January 1861 Mississippi, having declared its independence from the United States only 17 days earlier, adopted a new flag. It was white, with a five-pointed white star in the blue canton. A magnolia tree in natural colours was painted or embroidered on the white field, while a red fringe was sewn to the fly end. Some flags made basically to meet this description, or incorporating most of it, were carried by Mississippi troops. However, most carried the flags that were regulation to the Army or Department in which they served.

Missouri

In early 1861 orders went out to the Missouri State Guard, commanded by the pro-Southern Sterling Price, that each regiment was to have a blue merino flag with the state seal in gold or yellow on both sides. Some of these units transferred into the Confederate Army, bringing their state flags with them.

The seal, according to Wells, was as follows: 'On a circular shield, equally divided by a perpendicular line, is a red field on the right side, in which is the white or grizzly bear of Missouri. Above, separated by a wavy or curved line, is a white or silver crescent on an azure field. On the left, on a white field, are the arms of the United States. A band surrounds the escutcheon on which are the words, "United we stand, divided we fall." For the crest, over a yellow or golden helmet, full faced and grated with six bars, is a silver star; and above it, a constellation of twenty-three smaller stars. The supporters are two grizzly bears, standing on a scroll inscribed *Salus populi suprema lex esto*—"The public safety is the supreme law." '

New Hampshire

Although there was no official state flag in 1861, state militia troops had used as early as 1792 a blue flag with the state seal on both sides. However, in 1861 regimental colors issued by the state to its regiments were white, with yellow fringe and blue and white cords and tassels. The Arms of the United States were painted on the obverse and the state seal on the reverse.

According to Wells, the seal featured 'A circular field, surrounded by a laurel wreath, encompassed by the words, in Roman capitals, *Sigitlum Reipublicae Neo Hantomensis*: "The Seal of the State of New-Hampshire," with the date, 1784, indicating the time of the adoption of the State Constitution. Land and water are represented in the foreground, with the trunk of a tree on which the hardy woodman is yet engaged, embracing a scene of busy life, significant of the industrious habits of the people; and a ship on the stocks, just ready for launching, with the American banner displayed, is figurative of the readiness to embark on the sea of political existence. The sun, just emerging above the horizon, symbolizes the rising destiny of the State.'

New Jersey

New Jersey's troops carried both regimental and national colors bearing the state seal. Most issued national colors had the state seal painted in the canton, surrounded by a five-pointed star for each state in the United States. These were made by the

The 47th North Carolina Infantry Regiment carried this version of the state flag. The black number in the centre of the star is a US War Department capture number. (North Carolina Museum of History)

Philadelphia firms of Evans & Hassall and Horstmann, and were very similar to Pennsylvania's state national colors. While the US Army regimental color was supposedly the issued pattern, a number of regiments, such as the 12th and 36th Infantry, received dark blue regimental colors with the state seal within a large oval above the regimental designation in a red scroll. Many also bore an inscription on the red scroll from the presenting body, such as 'Presented/by the Sunday School Army/of Burlington County/To the 33rd Regiment N. Jersey Volunteers 1863.'

New Jersey's seal, according to Wells, had 'A white shield, or escutcheon, bearing three ploughs, indicating that the chief reliance of the people is upon agriculture. The crest is a horse's head, supported by a full-face, six-barred helmet, resting on a vase—the latter resting on the top of the escutcheon. The supporters are the Goddess of Liberty on the right, with her wand and cap, her left arm resting on the escutcheon; and Ceres on the left, her right hand resting on the escutcheon and her left supporting a cornucopia, filled with fruits and flowers.'

New York

According to the General Regulations for the *Military Forces of the State of New York* (Albany, 1858):

'718. Each regiment of Artillery shall have two colors. The first, or national color, of stars and stripes, as described for the national flag, and may be either of silk or bunting, with red cord and tassles. The second or regimental color, to be of yellow silk, with the arms of the State of New-York embroidered in silk on the center, over two cannon crossing, with the number of the regiment above and the letters N.Y.S.M. below their intersection. The cannons, regimental numbers and letters to be in gold embroidery, fringe gold or yellow silk four inches deep. Each color to be six feet six inches fly, and six feet deep on the pike. The pike, including the eagle and ferule, to be nine feet ten inches in length. Cords and tassels, red and yellow silk intermixed.

'Colors of infantry and rifle regiments: 719. Each regiment of infantry or rifles shall have two colors. The first, or national color, of stars and stripes, as described for the national flag, and may be either of silk or bunting, with red cord and tassels. The second, or regimental color, to be of blue silk, with

The state flag carried by the 48th North Carolina Infantry Regiment had battle honours printed in black on white stripes applied diagonally across its face. (North Carolina Museum of History)

The reverse of the state flag carried by the 48th North Carolina has different battle honours than those on the obverse. The bottom honours read, from the left, FARMVILLE, HATCHER'S RUN and REAM'S STATION. (North Carolina Museum of History)

the arms of the State of New-York embroidered in silk on the center. The number and name of the regiment, and the letters N.Y.S.M., in gold embroidery underneath the arms. The size of each color to be six feet six inches fly, and six feet deep on the pike. The length of the pike, including the eagle and ferule, to be nine feet ten inches. The fringe gold or yellow silk, four inches deep; cord and tassels; blue and white silk intermixed.

'Camp colors: 720. The camp colors are of silk or bunting, eighteen inches square; white for infantry or rifles, and red for artillery, with the number of the regiment on them. The pole eight feet long.

A plain dark blue flag with a state seal in its centre was also used as a state flag by North Carolina troops. This example was carried by the 4th North Carolina Infantry Regiment. (North Carolina Museum of History)

'Standards and guidons of mounted regiments: 721. Each regiment will have a silken standard, and each company a silken guidon. The standard to bear the arms of the State of New-York, embroidered in silk on a blue ground, with the number and name of the regiment, and the letters N.Y.S.M. in gold embroidery underneath the arms. The flag of the standard to be two feet five inches wide, and two feet three inches on the lance, and to be edged with gold or yellow silk fringe.

'722. The flag of the guidon is swallow-tailed, three feet five inches from the lance to the end of the swallow-tail; fifteen inches to the fork of the swallow-tail, and two feet three inches on the lance. To be half red and half white, dividing at the fork, the red above. On the red, the letters N.Y.S.M. in white; and on the white, the letter of the company in red. The lance of the standards and the guidons to be nine feet long, including the spear and ferule.

'Every pike-pole or staff to which the flags, standards, guidons or colors above provided are to be attached, will be surmounted with a gilt eagle.'

The state seal, according to Wells, had 'A shield, or escutcheon, on which is represented the rising sun, with a range of hills and water in the foreground. Above the shield, for the crest, is a wreath surmounted by a half globe, on which rests a startled eagle, with wings outstretched. For the supporters of the shield, on the right is represented the figure of Justice, with the sword in one hand, and the scales in the other; and on the left, the Goddess of Liberty, with the wand and cap in her left hand, and the olive branch of peace in her right. Below the shield is the motto, *Excelsior*—'More elevated''—denoting that the course of the state is *onward* and *higher*.'

Not all New York flags conformed to the printed regulations. The presentation flag of e.g. 20th New York State Troops featured a yellow field, with blue scrolls on which the regimental designation was printed, with the state seal in gold. Presentation flags carried by e.g. the 8th and 13th New York Cavalry Regiments had dark blue fields, but bore embroidered national eagles of various designs instead of the state seal.

North Carolina

North Carolina's troops tended to carry state flags more than did troops from other Southern states, but these varied widely in style.

The official state flag was adopted on 22 June 1861. It featured 'a red field with a white star in the center, and with the inscription above the star, in a semi-circular form, of "May 20th, 1775", and below the star, in a semi-circular form, of "May 20th, 1861". That there shall be two bars of equal width, and the length of the field shall be equal to the bar, the width of the field being equal to both bars; the first bar shall be blue, and the second shall be white; and the length of the flag shall be one-third more than its width.' The 1775 date is that of a supposed declaration of independence at Mecklenburg, North Carolina, while the 1861 date marked the date of the state's secession.

The first military variations of the silk state flag that were issued lacked the star and dates in the red bar along the hoist. Instead they were elaborately painted with blue ribands edged in gold, with a gold edging around the red bar. The unit designation was painted in gold on the blue ribands, e.g. 8th REG'T/N. CAROLINA/STATE TROOPS. These flags were made between September and November of 1861 and went to the first eight state infantry regiments, and the 1st Artillery, 1st Cavalry, and 1st Volunteer Infantry regiments.

Surviving examples of the bunting state flags made after November more closely match the regul-

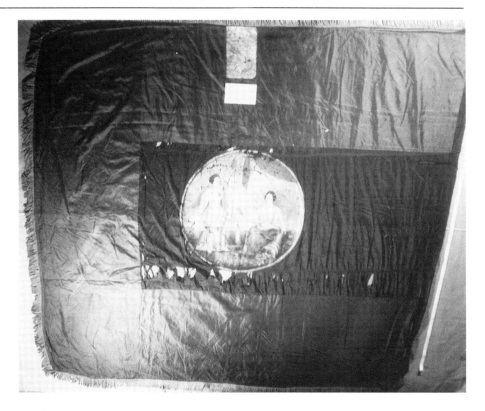

ation state flag. They have the regimental designations embroidered in white thread which matches that used on the dates along the bottom near the hoist, e.g. 34th Regt. NCV. These were made at the Raleigh, North Carolina, Clothing Depot, and were carried by the state's infantry regiments numbered as high as the 47th.

However, a number of state troop infantry regiments, such as the 4th and 6th Regiments, North Carolina State Troops, carried yet another variation of state flag. This had a dark blue field with the state seal painted in natural colours in the centre. Most had the unit designation as well as the seal, e.g. 4th REGIMENT OF/NORTH CAROLINA VOLUNTEERS, which appeared on a dark grey backing on the obverse, while the seal was on the reverse. On the flag carried by the 6th the seal was again embroidered on the reverse, while the obverse was embroidered in white MAY 20th 1776/NORTH CAROLINA/DEEDS NOT WORDS/MAY 20th, 1861. The designation SIXTH REGIMENT/STATE TROOPS appeared on a riband, or scroll, under the seal on the reverse.

According to Wells, 'In the original seal . . . on a white or silver field are represented the Goddess of Liberty on the right, and Ceres, the Goddess of corn and of harvests on the left. In the right hand of the former is a scroll, representing the Declaration of Independence, and the left supports her wand, surmounted by the cap of liberty. Ceres has in her right hand three heads of ears of wheat, and in her left the cornucopia or horn of plenty, filled with the products of the earth. In the background is a marine view, indicative of the commercial resources of the State.'

Ohio

According to the state's 1859 regulations, reprinted in 1861, Ohio units were to carry flags which were similar to those of the US Army save that the state seal was used instead of the national one. A gilt eagle was to top each pole or pike. Therefore, the blue infantry regimental color was: 'blue, with the arms of the State embroidered in silk on the center, and the letters O.V.M. (Ohio Volunteer Militia) beneath. The name of the regiment in a scroll, underneath . . .'

Artillery regimental colors were 'yellow . . . bearing in the centre two cannon crossing, with the arms of the State embroidered on the centre, with the letters O.V.M. above, and the number of the regi-

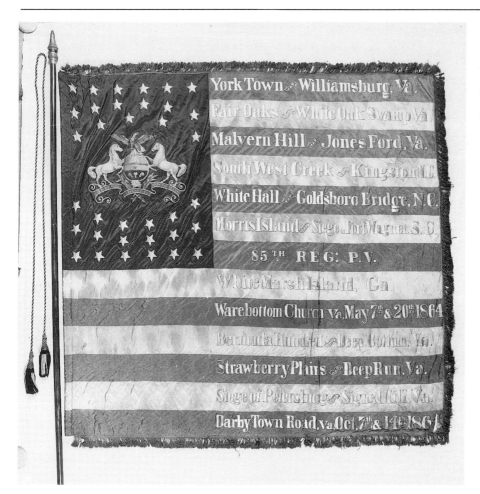

ment below.' The cavalry standard had 'the arms of the State, embroidered in silk, on a blue ground, with the number and name of the regiment, and the letters O.V.M. in a scroll underneath the arms.' The standard measured 2 ft. 5 ins., by 2 ft. 3 ins., with a yellow silk fringe.

Cavalry and light artillery guidons had 'to be half red and half white ... the red above. On the red, the letters O.V.M. in white; and on the white, the letter of the company in red.'

The state's seal or 'arms' featured, according to Wells, 'in a circular field ... several devices, significant of the general surface, business, and prospects of the State. The central portion represents a cultivated country, with the emblem of agriculture (a wheatsheaf) on the right, and on the left a bundle of seventeen arrows, indicating the number of States then constituting the Union. In the distance is a range of mountains, the base skirted by a tract of woodland. The rising sun, which is just becoming visible above

the mountains, betokens the rising glory of the State. The foreground is an expanse of water, with a keelboat on its surface, indicative of inland trade.'

On 19 August 1863 the state adjutant general ordered that: 'Volunteer regiments, battalions and squadrons will inscribe on their colors their proper numerical designation and the arm of the service to which they belong, with the letters O.V.M. They may also wear upon their colors the name of their city or county, or both.'

The placement of the unit designation varied according to the flag maker. For example, the 46th Ohio Veteran Volunteer Infantry Regiment had two national colors with a unit designation on them. On one the designation 46th, OHIO V.V.I. was painted in the canton, while on the other the designation 46 REGT. O.V.V.I. was painted on the second red stripe from the top. Unit designations on US Army regulation regimental colors were generally painted on the riband under the eagle, e.g. 60TH REG'T.

O.V.I. for the 60th Ohio Volunteer Infantry Regiment.

Pennsylvania

On 16 May 1861 Pennsylvania's legislature directed the governor to 'procure regimental standards, to be inscribed with the numbers of those regiments respectively, on which shall be painted the arms of this Commonwealth, and the names of the actions in which the said regiments distinguished themselves.' The state's adjutant general placed orders for regulation US Army flags, except that the state seal was to be placed on the canton of the national color, with 34 stars arranged symmetrically around the seal. The seal was also to appear on cavalry standards and guidons. Every unit raised in Pennsylvania received at least one of these state colors, except for the 154th (only a battalion in strength), 186th, 196th, 197th, 198th, 199th, and 215th Infantry Regiments and the 19th, 20th, 21st, and 22d Cavalry Regiments.

In the state seal, wrote Wells, 'On a white field is an escutcheon parted by a yellow or golden band or girdle, on which is represented a plough in its natural color. In the upper part of the shield, a ship under full sail is gliding smoothly over the waves of the sea, which are surmounted by an azure sky. At the lower part, on a green ground, are three golden sheaves of wheat, denoting that agriculture as well as commerce, is one of the primary reliances of the State. On the right of the shield is a stalk of maize, and on the left an olive branch. For the crest, on a wreath of olive flowers, is perched a bald eagle, with wings extended, holding in its beak a label, with the motto, "Virtue, Liberty, and Independence." '

Rhode Island

Rhode Island did not have an official flag, although colors bearing elements of the state seal, a fouled anchor under the word HOPE in a riband, do appear to have been used from time to time.

South Carolina

On 26 January 1861 the state's legislature adopted a plain blue flag bearing a white crescent, points towards the top hoist corner, in the area where the canton would normally appear. In the centre of the field was a white oval extending from top to bottom, with a palmetto tree painted or embroidered in natural colours, although the committee adopted 'a golden Palmetto, upright'. On 28 January this was modified to a simple white palmetto tree on a dark blue field.

Several regiments in the Charleston, South Carolina, garrison adopted a color whose design had been suggested for the Confederate national color in the *Charleston Mercury* in March 1862. This had a white field, quartered, with the top and bottom quarter in red. A blue shield with a white border edged with a narrow blue border was placed in the centre where the four quarters met. The white letters

Sergeant Alexander Rogers holds the first state color of the 83d Pennsylvania Volunteer Infantry Regiment, which was presented in December 1861. Sergeant Rogers was promoted to sergeant in the winter of 1862–63 and the flag was retired in the summer of 1863. (Ronn Palm collection)

There were two major manufacturers of national colors for Pennsylvania's infantry regiments: Horstmann & Brothers and Evans & Hassall, both of Philadelphia. Both featured painted state seals in their cantons, but there were slight variations between the flags each company made. Horstmann cantons measured about $38\frac{1}{2}$ inches by $24\frac{1}{2}$ inches, while those made by Evans & Hassall measured $38\frac{1}{2}$ by $29\frac{1}{2}$. Evans & Hassall's star arrangement in the cantons tended to be 6-6-5 over the seal and 5-6-6 under it, for 34 stars; and 6-6-5 over the seal and 6-6-6 under it, or 5-6-6 over the seal and 6-6-6 under it, for 35 star flags. Horstmann used 5-6-7 over the seal and 5-6-5 under it for a short time from September 1861, subsequently changing to 5-6-6-seal-6-6-5 for 34 star flags. Then it switched to 5-6-6-seal-6-6-6 until

Regiment	Issue (date of issue)	Maker	Regiment	Issue (date of issue)	Maker
11th	1st	Evans & Hassall	49th	1st	Evans & Hassall
23d	1st	Evans & Hassall		2d (Fall '64)	Horstmann
26th	1st	Evans & Hassall	50th	1st	Evans & Hassall
27th	1st	Evans & Hassall		2d (Apr. '64)	Evans & Hassall
28th	1st	Evans & Hassall	51st	1st	Evans & Hassall
	2d (Feb. '65)	Evans & Hassall		2d (Apr. '64)	Evans & Hassall
29th	1st	Evans & Hassall		3d (July '64)	Horstmann
	2d (Feb. '64)	Horstmann	52d	1st	Evans & Hassall
30th	1st	Horstmann		2d (May '65)	Horstmann
	2d (Dec. '63)	Evans & Hassall	53d	1st	Evans & Hassall
31st	1st	Horstmann		2d (Mar. '64)	Horstmann
32d	1st	Horstmann		3d (June '65)	Horstmann (never used)
	2d (Dec. '63)	Evans & Hassall			
33d	1st	Horstmann	54th	1st	Evans & Hassall
	2d (Dec. '63)	Evans & Hassall		2d (May '63)	Unk (captured 6 Apr. 1865)
34th	1st	Horstmann			
	2d (Dec. '63)	Evans & Hassall	55th	1st	Evans & Hassall
35th	1st	Horstmann		2d (Nov. '64)	Horstmann
	2d (Dec. '63)	Horstmann	56th	1st	Evans & Hassall
36th	1st	Horstmann		2d (Spring '64)	Evans & Hassall
	2d (Dec. '63)	Unk (Captured 4 May 1864)	57th	1st	Evans & Hassall
				2d (Feb. '64)	Horstmann
37th	1st	Horstmann	58th	1st	Evans & Hassall
	2d (Dec. '63)	Horstmann		2d (Nov. '64)	Evans & Hassall
38th	1st	Horstmann	61st	1st	Evans & Hassall
	2d (Dec. '63)	Horstmann		2d (Mar. '63)	Horstmann
39th	1st	Horstmann	62d	1st	Evans & Hassall
	2d (Dec. '63)	Horstmann	63d	1st	Evans & Hassall
40th	1st	Horstmann		2d (Dec. '63)	Evans & Hassall
	2d (Dec. '63)	Horstmann	67th	1st	Unk
41st	1st	Horstmann		2d (?)	A. Brandon (?)
	2d (Dec. '63)	Horstmann	68th	1st	Horstmann
42d	1st	Unk (lost 26 June 1862)	69th	1st	Horstmann
	2d (May '62)	Special presentation		2d (Dec. '63)	Evans & Hassall
45th	1st	Evans & Hassall	71st	1st	Horstmann
	2d (Mar. '64)	Unk (lost)	72d	1st	Horstmann
	3d (Dec. '64)	Horstmann	73d	1st	Horstmann
46th	1st	Evans & Hassall		2d (Feb. '65)	Evans & Hassall
	2d (Mar. '64)	Horstmann	74th	1st	Horstmann
47th	1st	Evans & Hassall	75th	1st	Horstmann
	2d (Feb. '65)	Horstmann		2d (Aug. '64)	Horstmann
48th	1st	Unk (lost)	76th	1st	Horstmann
	2d (Spring '64)	Horstmann		2d (Jan. '65)	Horstmann
				3d (July '65)	Horstmann

mid-1864, when it changed to 5-6-7-seal-6-6-5. Flags made under a May 1865 contract by Horstmann used a 5-6-7-seal-7-6-5 arrangement.

Evans painted the regimental designation as REGt. P.V.; REG: P.V.; REGt. PENNa. VOLs.; REG: PENNA. VOLS.; and REG'T P.V. , with the number added in the appropriate location. Horstmann designations were at first REGt. P.V., while their later flags were marked REG: P.V. and REG'T P.V. for volunteers and PENNa. REGt. for drafted militia regiments. As colors wore out most three-year regiments received more than one color, so that they carried flags made by both companies at one time or another.

Regiment	Issue (date of issue)	Maker	Regiment	Issue (date of issue)	Maker
77th	1st	Evans & Hassall	105th	1st	Horstmann
	2d (May '63)	Horstmann	106th	1st	Horstmann
	3d (Apr. '64)	Evans & Hassall		2d (Dec. '64)	Unk (lost 22 June '64)
78th	1st	Evans & Hassall			
	2d (Jan. '64)	Evans & Hassall	107th	1st	Horstmann
79th	1st	Evans & Hassall	109th	1st	Horstmann
	2d (May '65)	Horstmann	110th	1st	Horstmann
81st	1st	Evans & Hassall		2d (May '64)	Evans & Hassall
	2d (Spr. '64)	Horstmann	111th	1st	Horstmann
	3d (Jan. '65)	Evans & Hassall		2d (Feb. '64)	Horstmann
82d	1st	Horstmann	114th	1st	Horstmann
83d	1st	Unk	115th	1st	Horstmann
	2d (May '63)	Horstmann		2d (Feb. '64)	Horstmann
84th	1st	Horstmann	116th	1st	Horstmann
85th	1st	Evans & Hassall		2d (Apr. '64)	Evans & Hassall
	2d (Dec. '63)	Evans & Hassall		3d (Apr. '65)	Horstmann
87th	1st	Unk	118th–137th	1st	Evans & Hassall
88th	1st	Horstmann	138th	1st	Horstmann
90th	1st	Horstmann	139th	1st	Horstmann
91st	1st	Horstmann		2d (Feb. '65)	Horstmann
	2d (Feb. '64)	Horstmann	140th–142d	1st	Horstmann
93d	1st	Evans & Hassall	143d	1st	Horstmann
	2d (Mar. '64)	Horstmann		2d (Jan. '65)	Horstmann
95th	1st	Horstmann	145th	1st	Unk (lost 16 June '64)
96th	1st	Evans & Hassall			
97th	1st	Evans & Hassall		2d (Unk)	Horstmann
	2d (Sept. '64)	Horstmann	147th	1st	Horstmann
98th	1st	Horstmann		2d (Mar. '64)	Horstmann
	2d (Mar. '64)	Horstmann	148th	1st	Unk (captured 25 Aug. '64)
99th	1st	Horstmann			
100th	1st	Horstmann	149th–157th	1st	Horstmann
	2d (Oct. '64)	Evans & Hassall	158th–169th	(militia)	Horstmann
101st	1st	Unk (captured 20 Apr. '64)	171st–179th	(militia)	Evans & Hassall
	2d (Spr. '65)	Horstmann	183d–184th	1st	Horstmann
102d	1st	Unk (lost 5 May '63)	187th	1st	Evans & Hassall
	2d (Apr. '64)	Evans & Hassall	188th	1st	Horstmann
	3d (Jan. '65)	Horstmann	190th–191st	1st	Evans & Hassall
103d	1st	Horstmann	200th–202d	1st	Horstmann
104th	1st	Evans & Hassall	205th–208th	1st	Evans & Hassall
	2d (Feb. '65)	Evans & Hassall	209th–211th	1st	Horstmann
			213th–214th	1st	Evans & Hassall

C.L.I., for Charleston Light Infantry, were placed on the shield of the flag of this description carried by the 27th South Carolina Volunteer Infantry Regiment, which included the old Charleston Light Infantry. This also bore a battle honour for SECESSIONVILLE placed in the shield above the unit designation.

The first color of the 1st South Carolina Volunteers was plain blue, with an elaborate embroidery of flowers surrounding the words, in an upper semi-circle 1ST REGT and a lower semi-circle S.C. VOLUNTEERS.

Tennessee

Tennessee had no official state flag at the war's outbreak; but on 25 April 1861, before the state had even officially left the Union, a resolution was put before the state senate to have a state flag adopted. This was to be the Confederate first national flag, with the seal of the state replacing the stars in the canton. Since the Senate Committee on Federal Relations felt it unwise to adopt such a flag before the state had even seceded, the resolution was never acted upon.

However, such a flag was carried, at least by the 18th Tennessee Infantry Regiment at Fort Donelson in 1862; it was also marked with a unit designation. A variation of the Confederate first national flag, with the state capitol building surrounded by 13 stars painted in the canton, was carried by the 32d Tennessee Infantry Regiment. Another variation of the Confederate first national color carried by Tennessee troops had the motto 'Our Right is Our Might' painted in the canton. So the senate's suggested state flag, and variations of that flag, were used by a number of Tennessee's troops.

According to Wells the seal had 'A white or silver circular field, the upper half of which is occupied on the right by a plough, in the centre by a sheaf of wheat, and on the left by a stalk of cotton. Underneath these emblems, extending across the entire middle of the field, is the word "Agriculture," denoting that the first reliance of the State should be upon the productions of the soil. The lower half is occupied by a loaded barge, with the word "Commerce" below the water, indicating that the prosperity of all may be promoted through this means. Over

The national flag of the 22d Pennsylvania Volunteer Cavalry Regiment was made by J.H. Wilson after the actual fighting was over. It is, however, a fine example of a cavalry version of the state color. (Pennsylvania Capitol Preservation Committee)

the sheaf of wheat are the numeral letters XVI., denoting that this was the sixteenth State admitted into the Union.'

Texas

Texas had been an independent republic from 1839 for almost a decade before joining the United States; and the flag that had been flown by the Republic of Texas became the flag of the State of Texas. This had a single white five-pointed star centred in a blue vertical bar running along the hoist, with two horizontal bars, the top in white and the bottom in red, running from the blue bar to the fly.

This flag was carried by a number of Texas units, such as the 1st and 2d Texas Infantry Regiments. That of the 1st Texas, made in Richmond, had only battle honours for SEVEN PINES in a semi-circle above the star and GAINES FARM in a semi-circle, the words in white, below the star. That of the 2d

Texas, which was made in Texas, appears to have had the word SECOND in a white semi-circle above the star, and the word TEXAS in a semi-circle below the star, which was also surrounded by an olive wreath.

Other Texas troops carried variations of the 'Bonnie Blue Flag, which bore a single star'. That carried by the 8th Texas Cavalry Regiment (Terry's Texas Rangers) had a blue field with a large white star, $9\frac{1}{2}$ ins. in radius, in its centre. Made of bunting, the 23 in. by 33 in. flag had the unit designation TERRY'S TEXAS RANGERS in yellow letters over the star.

The single white star of Texas was also used on regulation flags to indicate what state the troops represented. For example, a single white five-pointed star was placed on the centre circle, or 'moon', of a Hardee flag flown by the 6th and 15th Texas Infantry Regiment at the siege of Atlanta and battles of Franklin and Nashville.

Vermont

Vermont's state seal dates from 1821. On 20 October 1837 the state legislature adopted a state flag: basically the US national flag, with a single white star in the canton with the state seal painted or embroidered in its centre. However, most of the state's volunteer units received presentation regimental colors with some variation of the state seal worked on a field of a single colour, which they carried instead of the state flag. Most early examples of such presentation flags were white, but blue flags, like US Army regimental colors, later became more popular..

Vermont's seal, according to Wells, had 'A circular field, in the middle of which is a tall evergreen with fourteen branches—thirteen representing the original States, and the fourteenth or topmost the State of Vermont, supported by the others. Beneath a cloudless firmament, the Green Mountains are seen towering in the distance, and in the foreground are sheaves of wheat and a cow, indicative of an agricultural and grazing country,

affording the true sources of thrift and independence for an industrious population. The Green Mountains have ever been considered characteristic of the hardy race which inhabits that region. Around the margin of the field, in Roman capitals, the word "Vermont" occupies the upper half circle, and the words "Freedom and Unity" occupy the lower half.'

Virginia

On 30 April 1861 the legislature adopted an official state flag: 'The flag of the Commonwealth shall hereafter be made of bunting, which shall be a deep blue field, with a circle of white in the centre, upon which shall be painted or embroidered, to show on both sides alike the coat-of-arms of the state as described by the Convention of 1776, for one side (obverse) of the seal of the state.' Prior to this the state seal had been used on military flags, but the field had more often been white than blue.

The seal featured, according to Wells, 'On a white or silver field the Goddess of Virtue, the genius

1: 9th Massachusetts Light Artillery
2: Camp color, 108th NY Volunteer Inf.
3: Guidon, Co.G, 1st Penn. Cavalry

A

1

2

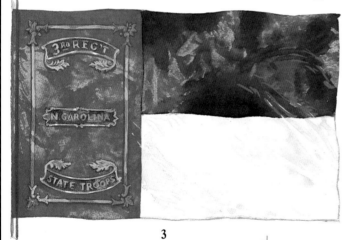

3

4

1: Co.E, 1st Maryland Cav. Regt.
2: 28th Virginia Inf. Regt.
3: 3d Regt. of N. Carolina State Troops
4: 1st Regt of S. Carolina Rifles

1

2

3

4

1: 6th Mass. Volunteer Militia Regt.
2: 33d Penn. Volunteer Inf. Regt.
3: 15th NY Volunteer Engineer Regt.
4: 7th New Jersey Volunteer Inf. Regt.

1: Georgia state flag
2: 1st and 3d Florida Inf. Regts
3: Alabama state flag
4: Co.H, 7th Tennessee Inf. Regt.

D

1

2

3

4

1: 20th NY Volunteer Cav. Regt.
2: 3d Massachusetts Vol. Cav. Regt.
3: Guide marker
4: Camp color, 56th Penn. Vol. Inf. Regt.

1

2

1: 3d Mississippi Inf. Regt.
2: Louisiana state flag
3: Co.K, 3d Louisiana Inf. Regt.
4: 1st Texas Inf. Regt.

3

4

F

1

2

1: 15th Wisconsin Inf. Regt.
2: 2d Wisconsin Inf. Regt.
3: 5th Minnesota Inf. Regt.
4: 1st Michigan Inf. Regt.

3

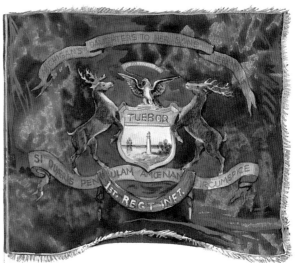

4

1: Co.A, 3d Mississippi Inf. Battalion
2: Co.K, 18th Mississippi Inf. Regt.
3: Co.A, 18th S. Carolina Hvy. Arty. Battalion

H

of the commonwealth, is represented, dressed like an Amazon, resting on a spear with one hand, and holding a sword in the other. She is in the act of trampling on Tyranny, represented by a man prostrate, a crown fallen from his head, a broken chain in his left hand, and a scourge in his right. On a label above the figure is the word "Virginia;" and beneath them is the motto, *Sic semper tyrannis*—"Thus we serve tyrants."'

Captain Charles Blackford, 2d Virginia Cavalry, described a mass presentation of Virginia colors to her troops in Centreville on 30 October 1861: 'We had a great display this evening. All the Virginia regiments in striking distance of this place were collected around one of the forts and the State flags were presented to them by Governor Letcher. I suppose we had some ten thousand troops massed and all the generals, colonels and staff officers, making quite an imposing show. The flags are very handsome and all alike, so every Virginia regiment fights under the same flag.'

Many Virginia troops appear to have used their state flags as their single color throughout the war, unlike most units from other Southern states. They are mentioned by at least one eyewitness at Gettysburg; while another eyewitness there mentions simply 'blue flags', which may have included North Carolina blue regimental colors as well as those from Virginia.

While, as Captain Blackford wrote, these flags were generally similar, there were some variations

Many of the first southern troops, such as these South Carolina militia troops occupying Castle Pickney outside Charleston just prior to the bombardment of Fort Sumter, carried plain blue flags with a single white star in their centres.

among them. That of the 2d Virginia Infantry, for example, bore nothing other than the state seal with the motto above the figures and with no unit designation or even the state name. One of those presented to the 28th Virginia Infantry in the mass presentation of October 1861 had the state name VIRGINIA in white letters on a red riband above the figures, while the motto in white on a blue riband was placed under the figures.

Eleven flags made in early December 1863 for infantry and cavalry of the Army of Southwestern Virginia by Rosaline Hunter and John Varni had the state name in a blue riband above the figures and the motto on a red riband below them. Letters were blue with white edging. The unit designation in red letters, e.g. 36th REGt. Va. VOLs., was placed on a white riband above the seal, while another white riband surrounding it bore battle honours in red.

West Virginia

West Virginia was created from what had been a part of Virginia on 20 June 1863, and its seal was adopted on 26 September 1863. While no official flag was named, the state legislature resolved on 28 January 1864 that the governor should present the 4th West Virginia Volunteer Infantry Regiment a flag 'adapted to their arm of the service' with 'the coat of arms of the state' and battle honours placed 'legibly thereupon'.

The South Carolina flag, as flown by this battery during the bombardment of Fort Sumter, was a plain blue flag with a palmetto tree in its centre.

The seal was an escutcheon bordered in gold, with a rock bearing the date 'June/20/1863' in its centre. On flags, the seal was simply a scalloped oval with the rock in its centre. To the left of the rock stood a farmer wearing a green hunting shirt with red fringe and holding an axe; a sheath of wheat and several stalks of corn appeared behind the farmer. On the right stood a miner in a white shirt and trousers with a red waistcoat, holding a pickaxe. Both men wore black hats. An azure sky backed the upper half of the seal; two crossed rifles and the cap of liberty lay on the ground in front of the figures over the motto *Montani semper liberi*, 'Mountain men are always free', painted in gold letters on a red riband.

This seal, painted within a scalloped oval, was placed on the obverse of the dark blue regimental flags eventually issued to all West Virginia infantry and cavalry units. On the reverse was a spread eagle holding in its right talon a sheaf of arrows and in its left an olive branch. The motto *E Pluribus Union* was carried on a riband that passed through the eagle's beak. The tips of the eagle's wings were 44 inches apart. The unit designation, in gold Roman letters, was placed on a red riband under the seal and eagle; and gold battle honours were also placed on the flags. The 6 ft.-square flags had gold fringes.

Wisconsin

Wisconsin's state flag, a variation of the US Army regimental color in dark blue with the state seal on its obverse, was adopted on 25 March 1862. The national eagle as per US Army regulations was painted on the reverse. On state flags presented as regimental colors to Wisconsin infantry and cavalry the unit designation was painted on both sides in gold on a red riband under the seal or eagle.

The seal featured a shield in its centre, with a smaller red, white, and blue national shield within

AN UNSURRENDERED FLAG.

BEAUFORT ARTILLERY, 1861 1865

that. A laurel wreath surrounded the national shield; a crossed shovel and pickaxe were at the bottom of the national shield, while an arm with a hammer was at the upper left and a plain anchor was at the upper right. Over the national shield was the motto *E Pluribus Unium* on a riband under a plough. At the left of the whole shield was a sailor in a black hat, white shirt, black tie, blue jacket, and white trousers. At the right was a yeoman in a red shirt, black hat, black breeches, and white stockings, holding a pickaxe. Under the shield were two cornucopia, while a badger appeared above the shield on a crest. The state motto FORWARD in a riband was placed above the badger. The entire seal was painted on a grey-blue circle edged in gilt.

Regimental flags bearing these seals were issued to Wisconsin troops beginning in 1863, through the state. Prior to that, issued regimental colors to the 1st through 8th Infantry Regiments matched US Army regulations fairly closely; but those from the 9th to the 19th (the last regiment raised) bore a blue scroll over the eagle with the gold word FORWARD. State seal regimental colors replaced these colors in 1863.

The first national colors issued to Wisconsin troops were made by Gilbert Hubbard & Co., Chicago, Illinois, and bore gold stars arranged 5,6,6,6,6,5. National colors made by this company in 1863 to replace worn ones had the stars first arranged 6,6,5,6,6,6, and later examples 6,5,6,6,6,6; the arrangement from 1865 on was in seven rows of five stars each.

US ARMY BRIGADE FLAGS

No special flags were authorised for brigades in either army. However, several brigades, through especially heroic actions or because of geographic uniqueness, soon adopted nicknames and personalities all their own. In the Confederate Army these included the

Stonewall Brigade from Virginia and the Texas Brigade. In the Union Armies there were Wilder's Lightning Brigade, the Regular Brigade, the Iron Brigade, the Irish Brigade, and several brigades bearing local designations such as the Vermont, the Excelsior, the Philadelphia (Pennsylvania), and the New Jersey Brigades. While the special Confederate brigades apparently did not carry unique flags, some Union brigades did.

The **Iron Brigade** was the only brigade made up of Western regiments in the Army of the Potomac. It was organised in the summer of 1861 with the 2d and 6th Wisconsin Infantry and the 19th Indiana Infantry Regiments. They were joined by the 7th Wisconsin Infantry Regiment in October 1861, and still later by the 24th Michigan Infantry Regiment. The brigade was assigned to I Corps.

In 1863 citizens of the states represented in the brigade then living in Washington DC ordered a special presentation color for the brigade from Tiffany & Co., New York. According to the *New York Times*: 'The flag is a regulation size and made of heavy dark blue silk. It is embellished by a handsome vignette of an eagle, shield and scroll motto, "E Pluribus Unium"—the same as on the ten dollar treasury note. The names of the principal battles in which the brigade has been engaged are handsomely worked, each on a separate scroll. The vignette, the scroll work, and the name of each regiment composing the brigade—the Second, Sixth and Seventh Wisconsin, the Nineteenth Indiana, and the Twenty Fourth Michigan—are all worked in the flag with silk chenille, and the shading is most exquisitely done. A rich and heavy border adds to and completes the effect. The staff is mounted with a massive silver spear head. The flag is a gift of a number of gentlemen from the great states of Wisconsin, Indiana and Michigan. It is a fit and elegant tribute to

The green flag of the 9th Regiment, Massachusetts Volunteer Infantry (the Third Irish), was presented to the regiment in June 1861. It was the first of three Irish flags. Note the gold shamrocks around the American eagle. (Massachusetts State House, Bureau of State Office Buildings)

the heroism of one of the most glorious organizations in the entire army.' Battle honours were placed on the flag for GAINESVILLE, BULL RUN, SOUTH MOUNTAIN, ANTIETAM, FREDERICKS- BURG and GETTYSBURG. It was presented to the brigade on 19 September 1863.

In November 1862, without orders, the 3d Brigade, 1st Division, Department of North Carolina adopted the designation 'The Red Star Brigade' and began flying a red flag with a white canton bearing a red five-pointed star. This flag lasted only a few months.

The only regulation special brigade flag flown within the Army of the Potomac was that of the 1st Brigade, 2d Division, V Corps, which was composed entirely of Regular Army officers and men. The Regular Brigade flag was originally red, from 24 March 1864; but on 30 April changed to blue, measuring some 18 ins. by 3 ft., with a white five-pointed star within a silver wreath on the field, and a silver fringe.

In the spring of 1862, during the Peninsula Campaign, the reporter George Alfred Townsend visited the Army of the Potomac's **Irish Brigade**. There he noted that 'Every adjunct of the place was

strictly Hibernian. The emerald green standard entwined with the red, white, and blue; the gilt eagles on the flag-poles held the shamrock sprig in their beaks; the soldiers lounging on guard had "69" or "88", the number of their regiments, stamped on a green hat-band ...'

The brigade, part of the II Corps, initially included the 63d, 69th, and 88th New York Volunteer Infantry Regiments. After sending off the non-Irish 29th Massachusetts, the brigade was reinforced by the 28th Massachusetts and 116th Pennsylvania Infantry Regiments, both also largely composed of Irish volunteers. It ceased to exist in June 1864, although a 2d Irish Brigade, with the same regiments save for the 116th and reinforced by several New York heavy artillery regiments, was created in November 1864.

The Irish Brigade did not carry a unique, brigade-wide flag; however, most of its regiments carried green flags, as Townsend mentioned, bearing Irish symbols—the harp and shamrocks. The one regiment which apparently did not carry a unique Irish flag was the 116th Pennsylvania, which carried only a Pennsylvania state color and a regulation regimental color.

US ARTILLERY BATTERY FLAGS

While the US Army regulations allowed flags to artillery regiments, there were none authorised for independent batteries. In practice batteries tended to serve away from a formal regimental headquarters, either assigned to corps artillery battalions, to support infantry organisations, or to artillery reserves. Yet, though other commands were able to put battle honours on their flags, artillery batteries had nothing to show for their histories, even though they had been authorised to do so by General Orders No. 19, Headquarters of the Army, 22 February 1862.

Volunteer artillery batteries first applied battle honours to their guidons, which were often of non-regulation design. However, batteries of Regular US Army regiments adopted an unofficial flag which was quite similar in design throughout the Eastern theatre. They were all generally some 3 ft. by 4 ft. with a 2-in. gold fringe. The field was red, save for that carried by F Battery, 5th Artillery Regiment, which was yellow. Battle honours were painted in rows on the silk fields in yellow or gold, usually in sans serif small capital letters. The design in the centre was a pair of crossed guns within a laurel wreath (not all flags had this wreath), with the Old English battery letter and regimental number arranged at the intersection of the gun tubes, as was regulation for the cap badge of the enlisted men. The letters US were intertwined on top of the gun tubes at the intersection. Often the Old English letters US were placed on either side of the crossed guns. Grommets or buttonholes were placed along the hoist side for attachment to a lance.

These flags first appeared in late 1863 and early 1864. Their use appears to have been limited to the Armies of the Potomac, the James, and the Shenandoah.

Table B: US Regular Artillery Battle Flags

Battery/Regiment	Variations from standard
K/1st	No wreath, white lettering
L/1st	None
M/1st	Battle honours in alternating yellow and black
B-L/2d	Gold cords and tassels
D/2d	No wreath
K/2d	No wreath
M/2d	No wreath, no letters US on side of gun tubes
A/5th	Wreath around flag edge, dates top and bottom, no US around gun tubes
F/5th	Yellow field

FLAGS OF THE US COLORED TROOPS

Although the first fighting units of black troops were created in late 1862, it was not until early 1863 that large-scale recruiting for these units—eventually called US Colored Troops—began. Eventually, there were some 145 infantry, seven cavalry, 12 heavy artillery, one field artillery, and one engineer regiment.

National colors carried by these regiments appear to have conformed to regulation patterns. Regimental designations were usually applied to the seventh bar from the top, although the national color of at least the 84th USCT Infantry had the designation 84th. REG'T in Roman letters on the top bar and U.S. Colored Infantry in script letters on the third bar from the top. Battle honours were painted on the red bars under that.

While the color sergeant of the 108th USCT Infantry was photographed with a regulation regimental color, some other regiments appear to have carried presentation flags. The 26th USCT Infantry had a blue silk flag with a gold embroidered oak wreath around the Old English letters U.S. over the Roman capital letters COLORED TROOPS. The gold riband over the wreath was marked 26th. REGIMENT, while that under it bore the motto GOD AND LIBERTY.

However, the most elaborate regimental colors issued to USCT Infantry were acquired by Pennsylvania for the regiments recruited in that state. Each one bore a different scene painted by the talented black marine and landscape artist David B. Bowser. The reverse of each blue silk flag apparently always included the national symbol over a riband bearing the unit designation, e.g. 3rd. UNITED STATES COLORED TROOPS. A riband above the eagle, which was placed within an oak-leaf wreath, bore e.g. PRESENTED BY A COMMIT-TEE of LADIES OF PHILa. OCt. 1863, or PRE-SENTED BY COLORED CITIZENS OF PHILADa. AUG. 31, 1863. The obverse bore the same oak-leaf wreath and riband with the unit designation under it. The scene within the wreath was different for each regiment, however, as was the motto over it.

Flaherty, Thomas, ed., *Arms & Equipment of the Union*, Alexandria, Virginia, 1991

Grebner, Constantine, *We Were The Ninth*, Kent State University Press, Kent, Ohio, 1987

Madaus, Howard M., 'The Conservation of Civil War Flags: The Military Historian's Perspective', *Papers presented at the Pennsylvania Capitol Preservation Committee Flag Symposium, 1987*, Harrisburg, 1987

Sauers, Richard A., *Advance The Colors!*, Harrisburg, 1987–1992

Todd, Frederick P., *American Military Equippage*, Vol. II, New York, 1983

Wells, John G., *Well's Illustrated National Handbook*, New York, 1864

Table C: Pennsylvania US Colored Troops Regimental Colors

Regiment	Scene	Motto
3d	Columbia presenting a flag to a black soldier.	RATHER DIE FREEMEN THAN LIVE TO BE SLAVES
6th	Columbia speaking to a black soldier in combat gear; a black girl behind him applauds.	FREEDOM FOR ALL
22d	A black soldier bayonets a rebel corporal.	SIC SEMPER TYRANNIS
24th	A black soldier on a hilltop receives emancipation from the hand of God.	LET SOLDIERS IN WAR BE CITIZENS IN PEACE
25th	A slave receives a rifle from the hand of Columbia.	STRIKE FOR GOD AND LIBERTY
45th	A black soldier holds a US flag in front of a bust of Washington.	One Cause, One Country
127th	A black soldier waves goodbye to Columbia.	WE WILL PROVE OURSELVES MEN

Sources

Cannon, Devereaux D., Jnr., *The Flags of the Confederacy*, Memphis, Tennessee, 1988

Crampton, William, *Flags of the United States*, New York, ndg

Flaherty, Thomas, ed., *Arms & Equipment of the Confederacy*, Alexandria, Virginia, 1991

THE PLATES

A1: 9th Massachusetts Light Artillery

The guidon of the 9th Battery of Massachusetts Light Artillery bore not only battle honours but the state seal. The 9th was in the vanguard during the retreat of the III Corps at Gettysburg on 2 July 1863, retiring by prolong, firing canister to save the battery guns. One battery officer was killed and all the others wounded; half the enlisted men were killed or wounded, and all the horses shot down at the limbers.

A2: Camp color, 108th New York Volunteer Infantry

This non-regulation camp color or guidon was apparently presented to the regiment after Antietam in 1862. The guidon measures 30 ins. by 17 ins., with a centre stripe 6 ins. wide. Then camped at Harper's Ferry, Virginia, the 108th received new regimental colors at that time from the 'Ladies of Brighton, Monroe County, NY'. The regiment served in the II Corps from August 1862 until being mustered out on 28 May 1865.

A3: Guidon, Co.G, 1st Pennsylvania Cavalry

The state-issued cavalry guidons incorporated the state seal with the company letter. This example was made by Horstmann Brothers & Co., and is the only one to survive of some 112 which the company made

under state contract. The 1st Cavalry carried blue state standards with the state seal over a regimental designation in a red riband. Officially the 44th Pennsylvania Volunteers, the 1st served in the Valley of Virginia in 1862 and thereafter was the Army of the Potomac.

B1: Co.E, 1st Maryland Cavalry Regiment (CSA)

The Winder Cavalry, later Co.E, was presented this standard by the ladies of Kent County, Maryland; it features the 1854 state seal in the canton of a Confederate First National Color. In the canton on the reverse is a circle of 11 five-pointed white stars with the motto HOPE IS OUR WATCHWORD, TRUTH OUR GUIDING STAR. The flag measures $27\frac{1}{2}$ by $46\frac{1}{2}$ inches.

B2: 28th Virginia Infantry Regiment

This regimental state color, made by J.R. Thompson

The 69th New York State Militia—a noted Irish regiment—was drawn leaving for the front 23

April 1861 carrying a green flag with a gold harp in its centre.

in Richmond, was presented to the regiment on 30 October 1861 as part of a general color presentation made to Virginia regiments located near Centreville, Virginia. The regiment lost almost half its officers and men at Gettysburg, surrendering three officers and 51 men at Appomattox.

B3: 3d Regiment of North Carolina State Troops

The first state-issued colors featured the basic design of the state flag, but with the regimental designation on the vertical bar; the silk flags measured 39 by 62 inches. The state insignia, with dates of 20 May 1775 and 20 May 1861 above and below a six-pointed silver star, is on the reverse. The 3d was organised in May 1861, surrendering only four officers and 53 men

at Appomattox after serving in all the battles of the Army of Northern Virginia.

B4: 1st Regiment of South Carolina Rifles

This $26\frac{1}{2}$ ins. by 46 ins. version of the state flag was made by Mrs. Alexander H.Mazyck and Mrs. Ellison Capers from two of their silk dresses (Mrs. Mazyck provided the white and Mrs. Capers the blue), with the gold lettering painted on. The flag was presented to the regiment on 4 October 1861, and was retired early. Also known as Orr's Rifles, the regiment went on to serve with the Army of Northern Virginia, finally surrendering nine officers and 148 men at Appomattox.

C1: 6th Massachusetts Volunteer Militia Regiment

This typical state regimental color was carried by the 6th when the regiment was attacked by a pro-Southern mob in Baltimore on 19 April 1861. The regiment was the first to shed blood during the war.

C2: 33d Pennsylvania Volunteer Infantry Regiment

The unit was raised as the 1st Regiment, Pennsylvania Reserve Corps. This is the second state color, awarded on 17 December 1863; the first one, presented on 10 September 1862, had been worn out in service with the Army of the Potomac. This flag, measuring 71 ins. by $77\frac{1}{2}$ ins., was made by Evans & Hassall.

C3: 15th New York Volunteer Engineer Regiment

As foot units, engineer regiments carried colors of the same style as infantry regiments. The 15th, one of only two volunteer engineer regiments in the Army of the Potomac, was given this presentation color, which was embroidered rather than painted.

C4: 7th New Jersey Volunteer Infantry Regiment

This national color was made under contract by Horstmann Brothers & Co., Philadelphia, for the state of New Jersey. The 7th was mustered in on 3 September 1861, serving in the III Corps until March 1864 when it was transferred to the II Corps. It was mustered out on 17 July 1865.

D1: Georgia state flag

This particular version of a Georgia state flag was presented to an unknown unit in 1861. Although there was no official state flag, examples like this with the state seal on a blue field are typical. At least one flag, however, used a red field.

D2: 1st and 3d Florida Infantry Regiments
The 1st and 3d Florida Infantry Regiments were merged in a field consolidation in December 1862, serving as one unit until April 1865. The unit served in the Army of the Tennessee when this interesting and completely non-regulation variation of the Army of Northern Virginia battle flag was created for its use. It is typical of the way that the official flag was redesigned in a number of different styles in the field.

D3: Alabama state flag
Best known as the Secession Convention Flag, this state flag was rarely carried by troops in the field because its complexity of design which made it difficult to produce. The reverse features a cotton plant guarded by a rattlesnake over the motto NOLI ME TANGERE.

D4: Co.H, 7th Tennessee Infantry Regiment
This silk flag, measuring 58 ins. by 90 ins., was presented to the company on its formation in 1861. It places the state seal where the canton would be; such a placement was suggested for the version of the Confederate first national flag which was proposed as the official state flag.

E1: 20th New York Volunteer Cavalry Regiment
This embroidered silk flag was made by Tiffany & Co., New York, as a non-regulation presentation flag for the regiment. It incorporates the colonel's name over the state seal. The regiment also carried a non-regulation national color made by Tiffany with the unit designation 'McClellan Cavalry' embroidered in script on the seventh bar, and '20th N.Y.V.C.' on the eighth bar.

An Irish Brigade flag, behind the mounted officer, is pressed forward in this 1861 illustration.

E2: 3d Massachusetts Volunteer Cavalry Regiment

The 3d received this painted standard on 21 February 1865 while it was camped near Pleasant Valley, Maryland. The flag was made by Charles O. Eaton of Boston. At that time the regiment was part of the reserve cavalry brigade, Army of the Shenandoah; prior to that it had been in the XIX Corps.

E3: Left general guide marker, 72d Pennsylvania Volunteer Infantry Regiment (?)

This painted general guide marker was owned by Thomas F. Longaker, who had been a lieutenant in Co. E, 72d PVI; it is therefore quite possible, but not certain, that this interesting flag belonged to that regiment of 'Fire Zouaves'. It is, however, typical of the wide variety of non-regulation guide markers and camp colors used.

E4: Camp color, 56th Pennsylvania Volunteer Infantry Regiment

By regulation, infantry camp colors should have been white with a regimental number on them. Many were actually dark blue, and state names were also displayed. The officers of the 56th PVI also included battle honours on their camp colors.

F1: 3d Mississippi Infantry Regiment

The 3d carried this state flag, which was made of silk, measuring 51 ins. by 74 ins., with a wool fringe; the tree is painted. The 3d served around Vicksburg, later being assigned to the Army of Tennessee.

F2: Louisiana state flag

This particular version of the state flag, which measures $47\frac{1}{2}$ ins. by 71 ins., was apparently an unknown unit's official color and was carried in action: the original, in the Texas State Archives, Austin, shows battle damage.

F3: Co. K, 3d Louisiana Infantry Regiment

The pelican feeding its young had long been the symbol of Louisiana, appearing on state buckles and buttons as well as flags. This silk flag, 61 ins. by 59 ins., has the motto SOUTHERN RIGHTS INVIOLATE within a laurel and oak leaf wreath, under the unit designation PELICAN RIFLES painted in gold on a dark blue scroll on the reverse.

F4: 1st Texas Infantry Regiment

This version of the state flag was actually made in Richmond in the spring of 1861 by the colonel's daughter, Lula Wigfall. Made of silk with painted

Left, above *The battle flag of Battery L, 1st US Artillery Regiment. (West Point Museum Collections)*

Left, below *The battle flag of Batteries B and L, 2d US Artillery Regiment. (West Point Museum Collections)*

Right *The battle flag of Battery K, 1st US Artillery Regiment, lacked the usual wreath. (West Point Museum Collections)*

Even national colors were often prepared with non-regulation designs. This national color was presented to the 17th Regiment, Massachusetts Volunteer Infantry Regiment, by the loyal citizens of Baltimore, Maryland, in March 1862. The portrait of George Washington on the canton was done in natural colours. (Massachusetts State House, Bureau of State Office Buildings)

The American eagle was displayed in the canton of the national color carried by the 24th Michigan Infantry Regiment. Note the axehead on top of the flagpole. (US Army Military History Institute)

battle honours, it measures 56 by $55\frac{1}{2}$ inches. The regiment was the only one of the Texas Brigade in the Army of Northern Virginia to carry a state flag, although they were common among Texas troops in other commands.

G1: 15th Wisconsin Infantry Regiment

The national color of this almost wholly Norwegian regiment incorporates the lion of Norway, on the red shield, leaning against the US shield. The motto means 'for God and our land'.

G2: 2d Wisconsin Infantry Regiment

The reverse of this flag, which was made by George Hubbard & Co., Chicago, is of the same design save that the US coat of arms, with the eagle and riband, appears within the circle on the centre of the field in place of the state seal. The flag measures 76 ins. by $70\frac{3}{4}$ ins., plus a $2\frac{1}{2}$ in. fringe.

G3: 5th Minnesota Infantry Regiment

This regimental color, which bears the state seal in the centre, was actually made by Horstmann Brothers & Co. in Philadelphia in late 1862. The regiment served in the Western theatre, against both Indians and Confederates.

G4: 1st Michigan Infantry Regiment

The state seal was used on a blue field, shortly before it became the official state flag, by the state's first infantry regiment. The regiment served first in the III Corps, later in the V Corps of the Army of the Potomac.

H1: Co.A, 3d Mississippi Infantry Battalion

Typical of the unusual varieties of non-regulation flags carried by early war volunteer units. This unit suffered greatly at the Battle of Shiloh and was merged into the 33d Mississippi Infantry Regiment. The thistle and motto suggest a strong Scottish element among the men, as does the original unit designation 'Duncan Riflemen'. The color bearer wears the final 1861 state uniform; earlier versions had red, and later green trim.

H2: Co.K 18th Mississippi Infantry Regiment

This flag has much in common with the state flag, especially the tree and white field. Measuring 42 ins. by 43 ins., it is of hand-painted silk. The regiment served in the Army of Northern Virginia, eventually surrendering just one officer, one non-commissioned officer, and one private at Appomattox.

H3: Co.A, 18th South Carolina Heavy Artillery Battalion

This crude variation of the South Carolina state flag was flown at the siege of Fort Sumter at the beginning of the war by the Palmetto Guards, which later became Co.A of the 18th. Also known as the Siege Train Artillery Battalion, the unit served around Charleston until the approach of Sherman's forces, when it was converted into an infantry battalion.